The Virtue of Hope

THE VIRTUE OF HOPE

How Confidence in God Can
Lead You to Heaven

Father Philip Bochanski

TAN Books
Charlotte, North Carolina

Cover design by Caroline K. Green

Library of Congress Control Number: 2019930531

ISBN: 978-1-5051-1418-8

Printed in the United States by
TAN Books
PO Box 410487
Charlotte, NC 28241
www.TANBooks.com

Printed in the United States of America

CONTENTS

To Live a Daring Life

L ife at the beginning of the twenty-first century can seem challenging indeed. I wonder sometimes how many people still have the courage to read the paper or watch the evening news when the headline and teaser to every story seem to reiterate a very limited vocabulary almost incessantly: *Crisis—Turmoil—Unrest—Violence—War—Poverty—Hunger—Disease—Addiction—Crime.* These realities may not be new (indeed, in many ways they are almost as old as humanity itself, for they are as old as sin), but all too often they affect our daily lives, our neighborhoods, and our homes, and they threaten to consume the little part of the world that belongs to us and to those we love. They leave us feeling overwhelmed, outmatched, even desperate. Small wonder then that during the elections for president of the United States in 2008, one of the most memorable and perhaps most effective political advertisements simply showed a stylized portrait of one of the candidates accompanied by a single word in bold letters: "HOPE."

But it is hardly coincidental that, at almost the same time, Pope Benedict XVI was addressing the universal Church with something much more substantial than a campaign poster, yet centered on the same theme. His encyclical letter *Spe Salvi*, which is translated "Saved in Hope," was written as an attempt to do what Saint Peter exhorts the early Christians to do in his first letter, tucked away at the end of the New Testament—"Always be ready," he says, "to give an explanation to anyone who asks you for a reason for your hope" (1 Pt 3:15). Writing at such a momentous time in human history—full of potential but also dealing with such difficult crises—the Holy Father used this encyclical to reflect on Christian hope and the way that it transforms and fulfills all of our individual, earthly hopes by placing them in their proper context. When we understand the reasons for our hope, the Holy Father seems convinced—when we know where it comes from and where it's leading us—then we will have the strength to persevere along life's road, however difficult our particular path may seem at any given moment.

This book has the same goal as Pope Benedict's encyclical: understanding the reasons that Christians have for hope and how to put that hope into practice. We're going to accomplish this goal in two ways because, as the Holy Father explains, a proper understanding of hope has to include two aspects. Of course, we have to appreciate the theological and philosophical foundation for what we believe about the Christian life and our relationship with God, because hope is a fundamental part of living out this relationship. We'll rely on Sacred Scripture and the teachings of the Church, especially as we can find them in the *Catechism* and the writings and homilies of the popes. We'll also rely on the work of saintly theologians and philosophers like Augustine and Thomas Aquinas, as well as some of their more modern interpreters, and we'll find that we can learn a thing or two from pre-Christian philosophers like Aristotle and Plato as well.

Just as important as this theological foundation, however, is the fact that, as Pope Benedict points out in *Spe Salvi*, "To come to know God—the true God—means to receive hope. . . . Hope ensues from a real encounter with this God."[1] Our pursuit of hope cannot remain something merely theoretical; it has to lead us to a deeper relationship with God, an encounter with the One who loves us and calls us to friendship with himself. As we consider God's plan for us, we are going to see that we are created precisely for this encounter and this friendship—it is our destiny—and that this is the reason that God gives us the virtue of hope in the first place.

Along the way, we are going to examine the lives of men and women—some from the early centuries of Christianity, some from our own day—who encountered God in moments of personal difficulty—sometimes in the midst of extreme crises—and in the process learned valuable lessons about hope. As we hear their life stories, and often their own words, these "heroes of hope" won't just inspire us. They'll also remind us that, as Pope Benedict once told an interviewer, there are "as many" ways to God "as

---

[1]   Benedict XVI, Encyclical *Spe Salvi* (November 30, 2007), no. 3.

there are people"[2] and that we, too, may find our way to an encounter with him as long as we hold on to our hope.

Defining Virtue

We should begin our discussion of the virtue of hope by examining what we mean by *virtue*. It's one of those words that we use quite often, without stopping to make sure that everyone understands the same thing when they say it. Sometimes we use it in a half-joking, chiding tone, reminding someone who's about to lose her temper that "patience is a virtue!" At other times, virtue and vice take the form of the tiny comic angel and devil on the shoulders of someone trying to make a decision—and in these depictions, somehow virtue never seems to appear quite as strong or quite as interesting. Whatever our preconceived cultural ideas of virtuous people or virtuous actions might be, we'll find that the classic philosophical and theological definition of virtue is actually quite specific and that each of its various aspects has something important to teach us as we learn how to become more hopeful people.

The notion of virtue can be found long before Christianity in the works of the great Greek philosophers, although they used it somewhat differently than Christians do today. For thinkers like Aristotle and Plato, virtue was equivalent to *areté*, a word that connotes "excellence" in the sense of "being fulfilled" or "living up to one's potential." *Areté* in this sense does not *necessarily* imply anything moral: A

---

2   Joseph Ratzinger, *Salt of the Earth: The Church at the End of the Millennium. An Interview With Peter Seewald,* trans. Adrian J. Walker (San Francisco: Ignatius Press, 1997), 32.

house that is in perfect proportion, symmetrical and beautifully adorned, has the *areté* of a house. The dog that wins
Best in Show at the Westminster Kennel Club does so
because he possesses the *areté* of his breed. A shoemaker
who makes really excellent shoes does so with *areté;* an
athlete who wins championships does likewise.

Of course, the philosophers did acknowledge a special
kind of *areté*, what we may call ethical virtues, that is necessary for human beings who live together in society and
therefore must work for the common good. Aristotle said
that these ethical virtues were found by striving for the
mean—the good quality that is the proper balance between
two vices, which could be considered opposite extremes.
Be neither cowardly nor foolhardy, he said, but find your
areté in courage; don't be stingy, but don't be extravagant
either: the proper measure is generosity. Achieving human
excellence, for Aristotle, meant learning to hit this mark
repeatedly, which requires deliberate choices and lots of
practice because the bad alternatives at either extreme
tend to be more attractive and usually require less effort.
But when one perseveres in exerting the effort, acquiring
areté brings great rewards. Not only does it make a person
able to contribute to and to do good in the society in which
he is living, but, more importantly, it leads to his personal
fulfillment and therefore his real happiness.

In his important work called the *Nicomachean Ethics*,
Aristotle lists a number of ethical virtues that he considered important because they helped a person to do good
and to be good in society; they include such things as courage, generosity, gentleness, friendliness, and truthfulness.

A few important things stand out about a list like this. First of all, no one can argue that qualities like these are important to getting along with other people; they are things that everyone ought to try to put into practice to some degree. Although we may be accustomed to associate them with a particularly Christian attitude—Jesus was certainly generous and gentle, friendly and truthful—one doesn't have to be a Christian, or indeed to have any religion at all, to see the value in these virtues or to put them into practice. In a very real sense, they are completely natural—we may simply call them human virtues—and plenty of secularists and atheists practice them, although their motivations may be different from believers who do the same.

There is a second point to be made about these human virtues, however. As natural as they may be, even self-evident and almost inborn, there is always room for development. Remember where we started with this discussion of *aretĕ:* it is related to fulfillment, which implies striving toward a goal. This is clear when we are talking about forms of excellence that are not related to morals or ethics; for example, the *aretĕ* of a musician or a baseball player. Some people are born with a certain measure of natural talent—indeed, some children have so much innate ability that we call them prodigies. Others have to work step-by-step to develop each and every skill. But even inborn abilities only go so far, and neither the "natural" nor the slow learner are getting anywhere near the perfection of *aretĕ* without practice.

The same goes for the virtues. Some people may be more generous by nature; others may find that they have an innate capacity for friendship. These human virtues come easily to them, to a certain degree. But the nature of a virtue, as we have seen, implies striving toward the goal of human perfection so that whether a particular virtue comes naturally or goes against our inclinations, it must be acquired by deliberate effort, like the musician practicing her scales or the athlete working on his pitch. Perhaps this is part of the reason that the ancient Romans used the word *virtus* to translate the Greek word *aretē*. *Virtus* is derived from *vir*, the Latin word for male or masculine, and thus connotes something strong or powerful. It takes a great deal of strength to persevere in acquiring the virtues, and to exercise them day by day.

How are the virtues to be developed, whatever their source? Let's go back to the beginning of our discussion of *aretē*—we said that it doesn't necessarily apply only to moral qualities but could connote any sort of excellence. Well, how does an architect construct a building with *aretē*? By studying the laws of proportion, learning about building materials and techniques, comparing structures to see what they have in common, and most importantly by trial and error, he eventually moves from building crooked walls to straighter ones, to solid houses and great masterpieces that embody the ideal of what a building ought to be.

How does a champion breeder arrive at a specimen that wins Best in Show, that has the *aretē* of its breed? By carefully selecting pairs of dogs; looking for the best, most ideal characteristics in their offspring; setting aside those offspring with less desirable traits; and continuing this process over several generations with dedicated attention and focus. How does a baseball player develop the *areté* that's equivalent to excellence in his sport? By breaking down complex maneuvers into their basic components and mastering them one at a time, then doing them over and over and over again until the mind and the muscles develop memory and endurance and can carry out the required tasks more and more efficiently.

The same approach is going to apply to the ethical virtues. Although the particular kind of *areté* that we are talking about—courage, for example, or kindness or truthfulness—may not seem as tangible as a pitch or a dog or a house, this shouldn't lead us to think that pursuing these virtues is something simply theoretical, something that's all in the mind. The ancient concept of *areté* makes it clear that even the ethical virtues—maybe especially the ethical virtues—are acquired and perfected in very practical ways; we learn by doing.

A person doesn't become courageous simply by thinking brave thoughts. Rather, he or she has to make an effort to actually be brave in concrete situations that require bravery. This is no small task since the very fact that bravery is required means that the person is probably scared—indeed, that the situation itself is inherently scary. So, like the architect who first builds a few crooked walls before he learns to build straight ones, a person trying to learn to be brave might miss the mark, probably more than once, on the way to learning it. Like the athlete developing his skills, the person acquiring ethical virtues will need to start small and do what's possible over and over, building both endurance and memory in the process. Like the breeder bringing out good traits and getting rid of bad ones, he'll need to pay close attention over time to what works and what doesn't, trying to hold on to the positive and let it have more and more influence in his decisions and actions. The acquisition of virtue in this way is a process, one that doesn't happen overnight . . . but one that bears reliable results if a person is willing to put in the effort and stick with it.

There is one more thing that we should notice about this discussion of the virtues. So far, with Aristotle, we have been talking about *aretē* from the perspective of striving, fulfillment, practice, perseverance, acquiring, achieving. But all of this kind of language leads to one necessary conclusion. If we are striving, we must be striving *for something;* if we are looking for fulfillment, there must be something specific in which we are destined to be fulfilled. In other words, all of this discussion implies that there must be some goal toward which we are meant to be heading, and some standards or benchmarks by which we may measure our progress.

Aristotle says that the ultimate goal of our actions must be "the Supreme Good"[3]; however, he goes on to make it clear that the ultimate good of which he is speaking is the good of "politics"; that is, the good of the society. "For even though it be the case," he explained, "that the Good is the same for the individual and for the state,

---

[3]   *Nicomachean Ethics*, I.2. 1094a. *Aristotle in 23 Volumes, Volume 19,* trans. H. Rackham (Cambridge, MA, Harvard University Press; London, William Heinemann Ltd., 1934).

nevertheless, the good of the state is manifestly a greater and more perfect good."[4] This is a lofty sentiment, as far as it goes; plenty of systems of ethical thought have been built on similar notions that the reason that human beings should strive for virtue is in order to be good citizens, in order to be able to do good and to be good in civil society. It is a kind of moral philosophy that is readily accessible and readily applicable to any political system, especially secular and pluralistic societies like our own that desire not to promote specifically religious moral codes.

However, this means that for us, the ancient notion of virtue as *aretē*, and the "supreme good" as the good of civil society, is only a starting point and not the ultimate answer. Don't get me wrong: the lessons we have learned so far about how virtue works are extremely important as we go forward. But just as important for us to understand is the purpose that underlies our pursuit of the virtues, the reason and the destiny for which we were created and to which we are called by our Creator. In the next section, we'll examine the nature of this call, and we will see that understanding it makes all the difference to the way that we live the virtues.

Called to Communion

We were discussing the fact that the word usually used in classical times to translate *aretē* into Latin was *virtus*, a word that connotes power—in this sense, the powers or faculties that belong to a human being—intellect, will, the senses, strength and desire, and other such things.

---

4   Ibid., I.2. 1094b.

This was connected to the idea of the repetitive nature of acquiring a virtue—think of the athlete developing muscle memory by practicing the same motion over and over and over again. He uses his natural powers—his *virtus*—to acquire his skill. You'll remember that we said that the same idea applied to acquiring ethical virtues: to become courageous, for example, a person needed to try to do brave things, and to keep trying even though he missed the mark occasionally. If a person used his powers rightly, the philosophers concluded, over time he would develop them to the point that he could consistently do good and be good in society.

Thomas Aquinas, the saintly theologian and philosopher of the thirteenth century who did so much to shape the Catholic Church's theological mindset, often used a different word to speak of the virtues: *habitus*. This means just what it sounds like: for Aquinas and for the Catholic Church, virtues are *habits*—firm dispositions of the soul that guide a person's decisions and actions. In a certain way, a *habitus* is very much like a *virtus*. Both become effective by being exercised, by being put into practice repetitively in concrete actions. Yet there is a very important distinction. To say that virtue comes from the natural powers or faculties of the person seems to imply that the only thing necessary is enough willpower and strength to get the job done. The notion of habit means something else. As habits of the soul, the virtues act as a kind of supplement and guide to a person's own natural abilities and faculties, leading them in the right direction, keeping them on track, assisting them to accomplish things they can't do on their own. But it's clear that these habits come not from a person's own strength but from some other source.

There's an important reason that this is true, and it's related to the fundamental reality of what it means to be human. Right from the very start, right from the moment that our first parents were created by God, the Scriptures reveal that God had a plan for the human race—that we are created with a destiny, a call, a vocation. And right from the beginning, it is clear that this vocation is *supernatural*; that is, it goes well beyond our natural abilities to attain it on our own—sometimes even beyond our natural ability to comprehend it on our own. The goal to which God is calling us has always been out of our reach if we were left to ourselves, and God knows that, so he has never meant to leave us to ourselves. Rather, he has provided the virtues and called us to acquire them so that, as Aquinas says, we may follow God more steadfastly, more readily, and with greater joy.[5]

Understanding and appreciating our supernatural destiny makes all the difference in how we live our lives, and whether or not we look for the virtues and put them into practice. To discover what that destiny is, of course, we need look no farther than the first page of the Bible. The stories of Creation that are related at the beginning of the book of Genesis have a great deal to say about who God is and how he works. Through language and imagery that is

---

[5]   Thomas Aquinas, *Quaestiones disputatae de virtutibus in communi*, I. In *Disputed Questions on Virtue [The Hackett Aquinas],* trans. Jeffrey Hause and Clausia Eisen Murphy (Indianapolis: Hackett, 2010), 220.

very dramatic and sometimes shrouded in mystery, certain characteristics emerge: God has absolute power to accomplish his will; he is orderly and methodical in the way that he carries out his will; he always works for good, and the various parts of his creation are related to one another in a hierarchy and for a set purpose. Moreover, the Creation stories reveal the place of the human being in the plan and purpose of God the Creator. Placed at the pinnacle of God's visible creation, mankind occupies a unique status as the only visible creature who is created in God's image, and after God's likeness (Gn 1:26).

To be created in the image of God means to exist as a *person*: as a subject who is self-aware, as a "someone" who can know himself and can communicate himself to other persons. To be a person, therefore, is to be capable of *relationships*. Along with this tremendous privilege— and it is a privilege: even the highest animals do not have the personhood that we possess—comes a great responsibility. For to be created in the likeness of God means that our relationships must be *like* the relationships that exist among the persons in the Trinity: among the Father, the Son, and the Holy Spirit. These relationships are always a total gift of love: so complete a gift of self-giving, in fact, that the three persons exist as only one God, with one Heart, one Mind, one Will, one Being. Although we cannot hope to achieve that kind of infinite love, we are made to imitate as much as we can the generous self-donation of God who creates us to be like him.

So, as persons created in the image and likeness of God, we may say that we are *created for loving relationships*—that it is our destiny and our vocation to love. More than that, we are created for one another: in the very same verse that reveals that the human being is created in God's image, the Scripture says that "male and female he created them" (Gn 1:27). A later verse teaches us that God made man and woman for each other because "it is not good for the man to be alone" (2:18); here again we see that we are made for relationships with one another based on the love that we see in God and that we have received from him. This reality is so true and so fundamental to human dignity and human identity that the Second Vatican Council insisted that "man, who is the only creature on earth which God willed for itself, cannot fully find himself except through a sincere gift of himself."[6]

Aristotle said that the reason we should acquire the ethical or moral virtues was because we were pursuing what he called the "supreme good"—though by this he meant the "political good," the good of the civil society in which we are living. Christian moral theology has a different goal in mind. We also pursue the virtuous life in response to the Supreme Good, but for us, this Good is not a "what" but a "Who"—we strive to acquire the virtues in order to respond to God who created us according to a plan and in order to be able to live in conformity with that plan. To live virtuously still means to do good to others and to be good for others, but our motivation for doing so runs much deeper than simply a sense of fairness or even self-satisfaction. Rather, to live virtuously, to do good and

---

6   Second Vatican Council, Pastoral Constitution on the Church in the Modern World *Gaudium et Spes*, 24.

to be good in all of our relationships is to live in accord with our human dignity and our human identity. It is to do what we were created to do. We won't be complete, we won't be fulfilled, until we learn to do it.

Now, since the time that the first human beings were created and entrusted with this destiny, several significant—we might even say game-changing—events have occurred in the history of humanity. Our first parents were created perfectly good and in a perfect relationship with God and with one another. Then, as the Scripture relates, "by the envy of the devil, death entered the world" (Ws 2:24), when the Evil One tempted the first human beings to commit the Original Sin. This betrayal of trust in God led to the wounding of every relationship—with God, with one another, with the natural world, between the body and the soul—and the effects of this sin and the wounds it caused continue to spread in every human generation. But it was also the occasion for God to make his first great commitment to the human race: the promise that the Original Sin and its consequences would not be the last word and that he would send a Savior to set the world free from sin and the death that it had brought about.

"When the fullness of time had come, God sent his Son, born of a woman . . . to ransom those under the law, so that we might receive adoption" (Gal 4:4–5). When the Son of God became incarnate in Christ Jesus, he provided a new context for the virtuous life. "In all of his life," the *Catechism* says, "Jesus presents himself as our model. He is 'the perfect man', who invites us to become his disciples and follow him. In humbling himself, he has given us an example to imitate, through his prayer he draws us to pray, and by his poverty he calls us to accept freely the privation and persecutions that may come our way."[7]

At the Last Supper, Jesus makes it clear that the example he sets for us is not to remain something theoretical but is meant to be taken to heart and put into practice. "This is my commandment," he says to his Apostles, "Love one another as I have loved you." The next day he was going to show them, and us, just what that love meant, as he laid down his life on the Cross to save the world. To love like this is not easy, but, as we have already seen, God commits himself to assisting us to carry out his commandments. "Christ enables us to live in him all that he himself lived, and he lives it in us," the *Catechism* says. "We are called only to become one with him, for he enables us as the members of his Body to share in what he lived for us in his flesh as our model."[8]

So, whereas the ancient philosophers saw the moral virtues as something focused on the needs of the society, and acquired by individual desire and effort, Christian moral philosophy roots our understanding of the virtues in our God-given vocation to form loving relationships and insists that the way to grow in virtue is to attend to the example of Christ Jesus and to rely on his assistance. "The moral virtues are acquired by human effort," the *Catechism* acknowledges, but it does not stop there. When

---

[7] *Catechism of the Catholic Church*, 520; quoting Second
     Vatican Council, Dogmatic Constitution on the Church *Lumen
     Gentium*, 38.

[8] Ibid., 521.

the virtues are "acquired by education, by deliberate acts and by perseverance ever-renewed in repeated efforts," it goes on, they "are purified and elevated by divine grace."[9]

The virtues "are the fruit and seed of morally good acts,"[10] the *Catechism* continues. This remark is related to something that we have already seen: the fact that virtues require practice. In the case of moral virtues, the more that a person makes good moral decisions "under the influence" of one of these virtues (so to speak), the more solidified and ingrained the virtue becomes. As we learn by doing, the virtues can be the "fruit . . . of good acts" because the more consistently we choose the good, the more second-nature the virtuous choice becomes. "With God's help," the *Catechism* continues, the virtues "forge character" and become the seed of future good acts.

Of course, the kind of character we are trying to forge is very specific. I mentioned earlier that for the ancient philosophers, there were all sorts of more or less self-evident moral virtues that still apply today, no matter a person's particular faith (or lack of it). It is possible to be truthful or generous or industrious, or to practice any number of other virtues, from a purely secular, societal perspective. We have a different rationale, however; one that Saint Paul summed up rather well in his letter to the Philippians: "If there is any encouragement in Christ, any solace in love, any participation in the Spirit, any compassion and mercy, complete my joy by being of the same mind, with the same love, united in heart, thinking one thing. Do

---

9   Ibid., 1810.
10   Ibid., 1804.

nothing out of selfishness or out of vainglory; rather, humbly regard others as more important than yourselves, each looking out not for his own interests, but [also] everyone for those of others. Have among yourselves the same attitude that is also yours in Christ Jesus" (Phil 2:1–5).

All of those human virtues that Saint Paul lists in this passage—humility, generosity, compassion, mercy—find their motivation and their completion in the last line I've just quoted: he wants the Philippians to have the same attitude as Christ Jesus, to learn to imitate him. This is the reason that we acquire the virtues, and it makes a difference: we strive to be humble because Christ was humble, and therefore we can learn to be humble in the way that Christ was humble. And, as we have already seen, when this is our motivation and guiding principle, we can be sure that Christ is helping us to accomplish our goal.

Up to this point, we've been talking about the human virtues in general, using mostly examples from the kind of virtues that Aristotle wrote about. Within this generic category, though, there are some specific types of virtues that are worth mentioning. One group is called the "cardinal virtues." This term doesn't come from the bird or from the bishops dressed in red—instead, the name for the virtues (and for the bishops) comes from the Latin word *cardo*, which means a "hinge," like the tool that keeps a door in place. Both ancient philosophers and Sacred Scripture identify these four virtues as essential; the book of Wisdom says that "nothing in life is more useful than these" (Ws 8:7). The cardinal virtues are *prudence* (making choices in accordance with right reason), *temperance* (using pleasurable material things in moderation), *justice* (giving what is due to God, neighbor, and society), and *fortitude* (spiritual courage in the face of adversity).

The other category of virtue is one that we might call, unofficially, "relationship virtues" when we apply them on a purely human level to human relationships. We've seen already how it is fundamental to our identity and our destiny that we are capable of and called to make loving relationships. But certain virtues, certain habits of soul are required if real relationships are going to be possible. First of all, we can't be in a relationship with anyone unless we know who that person is, and that is not possible unless we have an ability to believe what that person tells us about himself or herself. Over time we develop an ability to accept what the person is telling us and to reveal more and more of ourselves to the other. Gradually we grow in our ability to trust and our willingness to be loyal and stick with somebody . . . we grow in what we might call *human faithfulness*.

Another necessary quality to human relationships is the ability to trust in another person's intentions and to believe that things will turn out well. No relationship can grow if one or both parties is always suspicious of the other's motives . . . there can be no cooperation, no real intimacy, no trust. Friends look for indicators that the other person has their best interests at heart, that the relationship is "going somewhere," and they give their friends the benefit of the doubt when things don't go exactly as planned. Little by little, *human trust and hope* develop in a relationship and are reinforced each time someone proves himself trustworthy by keeping his promises and following through.

Of course, the foundation of any relationship must be love. This is so much more than a feeling, however—it has much less to do with flowers and chocolate boxes and valentines and much more to do with the Cross and self-sacrifice and patience. For love, ultimately, is a choice, and like any virtuous choice, it is one that must be made and remade over and over and put into practice in countless concrete ways over the course of a relationship. But underlying all those little virtuous acts of love is a fundamental choice to make all of one's little choices based on a simple but demanding calculus: "What is best for the person that I love; even when that does not equal what is easiest or most pleasant for me?" In general, this virtue of *human love* is something that flourishes when it is reciprocated—concrete acts of love pass back and forth between friends, or spouses, or family members, and reinforce one another in the process. Love that comes closer and closer to being unconditional is heroic virtue indeed.

So, we are made for relationships, and in order to form and live relationships with one another that are based on sincere gifts of self, we have need of all of the human and moral virtues, but especially human faith, hope, and love. Still, of all the wonderful human relationships we may have during our lifetimes, even the most passionate, the most committed, the most Christlike, will pale in comparison to the one relationship for which we were ultimately created, and in which we will ultimately find our true fulfillment and our real happiness: eternal communion with God himself.

It is usually easy for us to see how the "vertical" relationship that we have with God can inform us about our "horizontal" relationships (i.e., those we have with other human beings). Because God is good to me, I ought to be good to others; because God has forgiven me so much, I must try harder to forgive others. But we don't often stop to think about how often our "horizontal" relationships can teach us about our relationship with God . . . after all, who created the human person, the human mind and heart and soul, and even human society, but God, who knew that he would become incarnate himself some day? And if we look closely, we see that most of the same "rules" that apply in our human relationships are applicable in our relationship with God.

Let's stop for a moment, though, to consider exactly what it is we're saying. We've spent a lot of time so far talking about our relationships with one another, and that's fine—we've got an instinctive sense of how they're supposed to work, and we're all in this together. And we talk about a relationship with God rather freely because we're accustomed to doing so. But we must not underestimate just what an incredibly dramatic thing it is—an almost disproportionately impossible thing, in fact—for us to say with a straight face that the all-powerful, all-knowing, all-present Creator of the Universe—who has angels and principalities and powers under his command, who created the heavens and the earth and the seas and all that is in them, who has planets and stars and protons and electrons to keep in order—that almighty God actually desires a relationship, a real friendship with us poor creatures. Yet that is in fact what we're saying—and what he is saying, over and over—and much more. And that gives context and purpose to everything that we do, and is the reason that we can hope and that we must hope. In the next section, we are going to consider the kind of relationship God is inviting us to and the way in which we can and should respond to him.

A Hopeful Response to God's Friendship

We've already seen that the book of Genesis tells us that God has something special in mind for us: that we are created in his image and likeness and called to imitate his love in our relationships with one another by making sincere gifts of ourselves. The moral virtues, especially the cardinal virtues, assist our human faculties and allow us to do good and to be good in all of our relationships so that we can live up to our human dignity and answer this call. Most importantly, our ability to trust both what people are saying (we might call this human faith) and their motives and actions (we could call this human hope), as well as our willingness to choose what is best for them out of sincere love, are fundamental for building real relationships. We learn to do all of these things by practicing them in concrete circumstances, and God blesses and purifies our efforts, strengthening us to do his will.

If this were all that it meant to be human—that God gave us the ability and the assistance to love in his name—it would give us great dignity among his creatures. But the

Scripture goes much further: after it relates the creation of man, it immediately tells us that God begins communicating with the first human beings. He blesses them and their relationship with one another, calling them to be fruitful and to share with him in bringing forth new human life (see Gn 1:28). He assigns them tasks to perform as stewards of his creation, to tend the good things of the world and to bring them to their fulfillment (see Gn 1:28; 2:15; 2:19–20). He provides for all of their physical needs with an abundance of food (see Gn 1:29; 2:9; 2:16) and shares his presence with them (see Gn 3:8). In short, he treated them, not simply as creatures, nor even as servants, but as friends.

The *Catechism* affirms this truth about human nature. "The first man," it says, "was not only created good, but was also established in friendship with his Creator and in harmony with himself and with the creation around him."[11] Our first parents were filled by God with all the blessings that they would need to be able to know, love, and serve him—what the *Catechism* calls "an original state of holiness and justice"[12] that included an innate desire for God and an ability to come to a knowledge of God through his natural faculties.[13]

Sadly, this state of friendship with God in which the human race was created did not last long. The Original Sin was a breaking off of the relationship, a denial of God's friendship, and the breach lasted a long time—indeed, we

---

[11]   Ibid., 374.

[12]   Ibid.

[13]   Ibid., 27, 35.

still feel the effects of it, as we each inherit a human nature that is wounded and inclined to sin. But immediately—even at the scene of the crime, so to speak—God promised our first parents that the Original Sin would not be the final word, that the broken relationship would not stay broken. As we have noted already, God promised to send a Savior, who in the fullness of time made his appearance in the Incarnation of the Son of God. And on the night before he laid down his life to pay the price for the Original Sin and for the sins of all human beings of every time and place, Jesus Christ told his Apostles, "I no longer call you slaves. . . . I have called you friends" (Jn 15:15).

The New Testament goes on to teach us that even this friendship was not all that God had in mind for the human beings he created. When he writes to the Church in Ephesus, Saint Paul begins with a hymn of praise and thanksgiving for all of the blessings that God the Father has bestowed on the world through Jesus Christ, and insists that these have been part of his plan from "before the foundation of the world" (Eph 1:4). It was then, Saint Paul says, that God "chose us in [Christ] . . . to be holy and without blemish before him," and that "in love he destined us for adoption to himself through Jesus Christ" (Eph 1:4–5). He expresses this truth to the Galatians as well, with words that are reminiscent of Jesus's own words at the Last Supper: "You are no longer a slave but a child, and if a child then also an heir, through God" (Gal 4:7).

So now we come to an ever deeper, more intimate level of communion with God—not content to leave us merely creatures nor slaves, not even simply his friends, he calls

us rather to become his sons and daughters through fel-
lowship with his only-begotten Son, Jesus Christ. The
Church calls this reality *filial adoption* since we become
God's children, and brothers and sisters to Christ, not by
nature but by God's own choice and initiative, by God's
grace. The *Catechism* explains that this adoption "gains
us a real share in the life of the only Son, which was
finally revealed in his Resurrection."[14] Saint Paul tells us
that the "proof that you are children" of God is that "God
sent the spirit of his Son into our hearts," and that the Holy
Spirit cries out to the Father from within us, using words
of tender love, "Abba, Father!" (Gal 4:6). Saint John con-
curs with him on this, writing in his first letter that "we
are God's children now. . . . This is how we know that
we remain in him and he in us, that he has given us of his
Spirit" (1 Jn 3:2; 4:13).

Hopefully we now have a sense of just how marvelous
is the gift that God is offering to us, for no other reason
that his own free choice, on his own initiative—we don't
deserve it, we can't earn it, we can't pay for it. But "God
. . . wants to communicate his own divine life to the men
he freely created, in order to adopt them as his sons in his
only-begotten Son," the *Catechism* insists. "By revealing
himself God wishes to make them capable of responding
to him, and of knowing him and of loving him far beyond
their own natural capacity."[15]

Such a marvelous gift demands a response, and God
makes us capable of making a response to him. We've seen

---

[14]   Ibid., 654.
[15]   Ibid., 52.

that being in a relationship with any human being requires certain moral virtues: trust on the level of both the intellect (to judge information) and the will (to judge motives and actions), as well as the fundamental movement of the will towards the good of the other person that is the basis for real love. These are the bare essentials for any relationship, and they are difficult and demanding enough to acquire no matter who the other person in the relationship happens to be. But when we are talking about a relationship with God, the problem is compounded. Even before the Original Sin, it would have been very difficult: our human faculties have always been finite. But now that we are affected by sin, both Original and personal, it is all the more difficult to believe, trust, and love God the way that we should. So, as usual, God has taken the initiative and solved the problem himself.

When we apply these three qualities—the intellectual trust which is faith, the trust of the will that we can call hope, and, of course, love—to our relationship with God, they take on an entirely new significance. Up to now, we have been talking a great deal of *acquiring* the various virtues—of making deliberate acts of the will to practice a certain virtue in order to develop and strengthen the good habit. It is possible to acquire a new moral virtue like this in various ways, even from "scratch"—to say to yourself one day, "I want to be more _____," and, through prayer and dedicated hard work, to accomplish the task over time.

Faith, hope, and love—when we are speaking about them in reference to God—are not like the other virtues.

They are literally "in a class by themselves," categorized as "theological virtues" because they pertain to our relationship with God himself (the Greek word for God is "*theos*") and because they are given to each person freely by God along with the gift of sanctifying grace. For this reason, the Church says that the theological virtues are *infused* rather than *acquired*—God provides them right away because without them we could not know him at all, and therefore couldn't be in a relationship with him.

These virtues are also called theological because of the way that they "work," so to speak; that is, because of what Saint Thomas would call their object. The best way to explain what I mean is to compare them with their human counterparts. I mentioned before that in every human relationship, we are constantly faced with choices as to whether or not we will believe what someone is telling us; whether we will put any degree of "human faith" in a particular person—be he a friend, a family member, a colleague, a teacher, a news reader or weather forecaster, or a stranger on the street. Typically, we make these choices based on a variety of factors: how long we have known the person, whether he or she has been known to be truthful before, whether the story makes sense and fits with what we are certain is true. As we get to know a person over time, these judgments become more and more automatic—we are growing in the virtue of human faith—but if a person should prove at some point to be unworthy of trust, then we may reevaluate our decisions.

It is not the same with our relationship with God. Here we are talking about a partner in the relationship who is fundamentally unique from anyone else we know. We do not primarily "decide" to believe in the truths of faith because they make sense to us; rather, as the First Vatican Council explains, we believe "because of the authority of God himself who reveals them, who can neither deceive nor be deceived."[16] So the theological virtue of faith is a habit, a stable disposition of the soul, that guides us to do two things: to believe in the truths that God reveals to us and, more importantly, to believe in God who reveals them.

The other theological virtues work the same way. "In this is love," Saint John says, "not that we have loved God, but that he loved us" (1 Jn 4:10); therefore, the theological virtue of love enables us to love God who first loved us, and to love our neighbor because God loves him and out of love for God. And the theological virtue of hope has the same two-pronged approach. Day by day there are many things that we hope for—some healthy, some not; some helpful, others distracting—in the various phases and dimensions of our lives. Hope as a human virtue strives to attain these things when it perceives them as good; hope as a theological virtue purifies our aspirations, organizing and prioritizing them relative to our ultimate happiness: union with God forever in heaven. Theological hope enables us to strive for this eternal beatitude as our main goal, our top priority, and to see it as something attainable and tangible. At the same time, we know that, by definition, eternal life and communion with God is not within our natural ability to grasp on our own. So theological

---

[16]   First Vatican Council, Constitution *Dei Filius*, 3.

hope enables us also to put our trust in God and to be confident that he will always, continually provide the help that we require in order to reach the goal that he has set for us.

To Live a Daring Life

I feel like I'm repeating myself an awful lot; how many times can I say that the life God has chosen for us goes beyond our natural ability? But there it is . . . it's a fact, and there's really no getting around it. How are we to react to it? There is, I suppose, the cynical view. We could resent the whole thing—say that God is essentially unrealistic or, worse, just likes messing with his creatures and has set us up to fail. We could pout and refuse to participate, yell about how the game is rigged and there's no sense in trying, since the deck is stacked against us anyway.

I suppose there's actually more than one possible cynical answer. We could also say that there's really no plan, no reason to worry about God's expectations or our abilities, because everything is predetermined anyway and there's not anything that we can do to change our lot in life. We can complain that freedom is an illusion and that all this talk of plans and invitations is only meant to make people feel better but doesn't mean anything in the long run.

Or we can take the Scriptures completely seriously and buckle our seatbelts—because the invitation to friendship with God, to adoption as his sons and daughters, to communion with him and life that lasts forever, has all been offered to each one of us—and answering that invitation, living that life, starts here and now.

Several times already I've had occasion to mention the saintly philosopher Thomas Aquinas. We'll hear more from him throughout this book, and we'll also benefit from the insights of one of his excellent modern interpreters, Josef Pieper, a German scholar and professor who has written numerous books, including works on the theological and cardinal virtues. In an essay "On Hope," Dr. Pieper notes that the call that we have received from God—the call to which theological hope is helping us to respond—requires another virtue; namely, magnanimity, or "greatness of soul": "Magnanimity, a much-forgotten virtue, is the aspiration of the spirit to great things. . . . A person is magnanimous if he has the courage to seek what is great and becomes worthy of it. This virtue has its roots in a firm confidence in the highest possibilities of that human nature that God did 'marvelously ennoble and has still more marvelously renewed.'"[17]

Dr. Pieper describes magnanimity as a prerequisite for exercising theological hope. If we consider what we have been discussing so far, I think we can see his point. The Scriptures tell us that we are chosen and called by God to be adopted as his children—surely this qualifies as a call to greatness, and this is the object of our hope. If we are not willing to seek what is great, if we are unwilling to become worthy of it, then we have little left to hope for, at least in a theological sense. On the other hand, if we have even a tiny bit of courage—enough to open our hearts up to the possibility of seeking and accepting what God is

---

[17]   Josef Pieper, "On Hope," in *Faith, Hope, Love* (San Francisco: Ignatius, 1997), 101; quoting the *Roman Missal*.

calling us to—then the virtue of hope will take us the rest of the way.

What would lead us to resist this call to great things? Dr. Pieper describes a kind of spiritual sadness, which the monks of the early Church called *acedia*, as "a lack of magnanimity." In a rather chilling analysis, he describes some reasons why a person might avoid responding to God's call:

> [*Acedia*] lacks courage for the great things that are proper to the nature of the Christian. It is a kind of anxious vertigo that befalls the human individual when he becomes aware of the height to which God has raised him. One who is trapped in *acedia* has neither the courage nor the will to be as great as he really is. He would prefer to be less great in order thus to avoid the obligation of greatness. *Acedia* will not accept supernatural goods because they are, by their very nature, linked to a claim on him who receives them.[18]

Sad to say, it seems that many people neglect or even reject God's invitation precisely because it is so great, because what he is offering to us places so many demands on us. Perhaps there are a few people reading this thinking, "This is sounding like a lot more than I signed up for; I'm not quite sure what I'm getting myself into." The truth is, acquiring virtue *is* difficult—it always has been, because it takes focused, repeated effort, usually over a long period of time. And the theological virtue of hope is

---

[18]   Ibid., 119.

no exception; Saint Thomas says that "the object of hope conceived broadly is a future good that is demanding but possible."[19] But we may find it easier to trust that it is possible if we keep a few things in mind.

First, we are not meant to arrive at the destination of our hope all at once, and we are not there yet. The fulfillment of our hope has been promised to us by Christ, but we are still on our way to attaining it. Dr. Pieper insists that this fact—that we are "on the way" to the fulfillment of our goal—is the most important thing to grasp, not only if we are to understand hope, but if we are to understand our own human nature. "It is astonishing," he says, "how many basic concepts of theology have a meaning in reference to the state of being on the way that is different from their meaning in reference to the state of total possession";[20] that is, of having achieved our goal. For one thing, being "on the way" is a constant reminder to us that there *is* a goal toward which we are tending: that our lives are not aimless but are heading in a direction that is defined by God's will and implicit in our created nature. As long as we are "on the way," we have opportunities to repent and receive forgiveness, we have opportunities to keep trying and to succeed with God's help, and for these reasons, we must not despair. As long as we have not yet reached the definitive conclusion, we have no

---

[19]   Thomas Aquinas, *Quaestio disputata de spe*, iv. In *Disputed Questions on Virtue* [The Hackett Aquinas], trans. Jeffrey Hause and Clausia Eisen Murphy (Indianapolis: Hackett, 2010), 220.

[20]   Pieper, "On Hope," 92.

right to rest on our laurels but must rather keep working with perseverance and striving to grow, and thus must not give into presumption or fall victim to spiritual sadness. And the thought of the eternal future that lies ahead of us, which we hope to attain and in which our hopes will be definitively fulfilled, is rejuvenating. "Youth is a cause of hope," Dr. Pieper says, quoting Saint Thomas. "For youth, the future is long and the past is short."[21] He continues, "Supernatural hope . . . gives man such a 'long' future that the past seems 'short' however long and rich his life. The theological virtue of hope is the power to wait patiently."[22]

Although the complete fulfillment of our hope is only to be found in eternal life, Pope Benedict, drawing again on the Scriptures—"Faith is the *hypostasis* [substance] of things hoped for; the proof of things not seen"—insists that even now we possess "something of the reality that we are waiting for" in hope. "Faith draws the future into the present," he writes, "so that it is no longer simply a 'not yet.' The fact that this future exists changes the present. . . . Faith gives life a new basis, a new foundation on which we can stand."[23]

"A distinguishing mark of Christians," the Holy Father writes, is "the fact that they have a future: it is not that they know the details of what awaits them, but they know in general terms that their life will not end in emptiness. . . . The one who has hope lives differently; the one who

---

[21]   *Summa Theologiae,* Ia-IIae.xl.6.

[22]   Pieper, "On Hope," 110–11.

[23]   Benedict XVI, *Spe Salvi,* 7, 8.

hopes has been granted the gift of a new life."[24] We know, as a matter of theology, as a matter of faith, that we have been granted the theological virtue of hope as an unmerited gift by virtue of our having been baptized. We've got it. Whether we understand it, whether we are practicing it, exercising it, developing it, or not, are different questions. What is obvious is that it is extremely difficult to live in the modern world with any semblance of serenity—perhaps even difficult to live here with any great degree of sanity—unless we learn to use well the theological virtue of hope which has been entrusted to us.

Above all, we must remember that we are not alone. In the remaining chapters, we are going to consider various aspects of the Christian life—conversion, vocation, suffering, prayer—in which we need to be able to exercise the virtue of hope in order to stay focused and make progress toward our goal of communion with God. We will benefit by listening to the stories and hard-won wisdom of holy men and women who learned firsthand that God is trustworthy and keeps his promises. They will give us, by word and example, an explanation for their hope. Reassured by their experience, we will draw new strength to persevere, full of hope, on the way together.

---

[24]   Ibid., 2.

We Dare to Change

Preparing for Conversion—The Blind Man of Bethsaida

In our last chapter, we discovered how the theological virtue of hope orients our whole life toward our ultimate goal, the supernatural destiny for which we were created and to which we are called—that is, communion, friendship with God, which has its beginnings in this world and its fulfillment in eternal life. Theological hope trains and assists us to keep our attention always fixed on this goal and to prioritize all of our other hopes and desires subordinate to it—to see things as God sees them and to keep them in proper perspective. Most importantly, it teaches us to rely on God for help in all of our needs and always to trust that, because he is fully aware both of our limitations and of the greatness to which he has called us, he has committed himself to helping us, by his grace, to reaching our goal.

Until that point, we are still, always, "on the way"— and so theological hope gives us the strength to persevere without losing heart. While we are on the way, the life of the disciple involves many trials that may make it difficult to hold on to our hope unless we understand how this important virtue can be exercised in each situation. Throughout this book, we are going to look at some of the challenges facing the disciple and learn through the experience of "heroes of hope" how this virtue can sustain us in each one.

Life with Christ—the communion and friendship for which we were made and to which we have been called—begins at Baptism, but it must be lived out day by day. Like any relationship, there will be ups and downs; as in any relationship, there may be times when we do not fulfill our obligations to the One whom we profess to love. For this reason, as the *Catechism* reminds us, "Christ's call to conversion continues to resound in the lives of Christians."[1] Conversion means a "turning"—we turn away from sin in order to turn to Christ; we turn away from selfishness in order to turn toward him and give ourselves freely to doing his will; we turn away from our own agendas, judgments, and priorities in order to be more flexible and responsive to his call. "This . . . conversion," the *Catechism* continues, "is an uninterrupted task for the whole Church who . . . is at once holy and always in need of purification."[2]

The work of conversion cannot be something simply external, but must penetrate deep into the heart, where it brings about "a radical reorientation of our whole life, a return . . . an end of sin, a turning away from evil, with

---

[1]   *Catechism of the Catholic Church*, 1428.

[2]   Ibid.

repugnance toward the evil actions we have committed."[3] Such a process can seem grueling, at least on the surface, and therefore can be unappealing to lots of people, especially when you consider that conversion must be a lifelong process. Who wants to spend a lifetime radically reorienting themselves? Who wants to spend decades attending to past deeds with repugnance—especially when the *Catechism* promises that conversion "is accompanied by a salutary pain and sadness"!? The superficial concern that conversion and penance are hard to do means that, for many people, they go undone for long periods of time.

And yet, if we are to be in a relationship with God, our hearts must be ready to receive his friendship: they must be purified, broadened, opened. In a word, we must be converted. How is this possible if our hearts are weighed down at the very prospect of trying to change? Our previous discussion of our supernatural vocation gives us the answer: God knows that we need conversion, and knows as well that we cannot seek it on our own, so he takes the initiative, in his mercy, and extends a hand to us to lead us back to him. "God must give man a new heart," the *Catechism* explains. "Conversion is first of all a work of the grace of God who makes our hearts return to him."[4]

The virtue of hope allows us to see that this is real and to let the truth of this statement change our lives. If God loves us so much that he will even reach out to us to help us to turn back to him, then truly we have no reason to doubt that he will help us in all of our needs. Indeed, this

---

3   Ibid., 1431.
4   Ibid., 1432.

is Saint Paul's definition of God's love in his letter to the Romans: "God proves his love for us in that while we were still sinners Christ died for us" (Rom 5:8).

The Scriptures are full of God's call to conversion; over and over he sends the prophets to his people to remind them to be faithful to the Covenant and to turn back to the Lord. At times the prophets speak forcefully, warning the people of dire consequences if they continue to transgress the commandments and to disrespect the Sabbath and the Temple. But at other times, the Lord speaks through the prophets with words of compassion, messages that still resonate with us today and give us reasons to hope in God's mercy:

> Wash yourselves clean!
> Put away your misdeeds from before my eyes;
>> cease doing evil;
>> learn to do good. . . .
> Come now, let us set things right,
>> says the LORD:
> Though your sins be like scarlet,
>> they may become white as snow;
> Though they be red like crimson,
>> they may become white as wool. (Is
>> 1:16–18)

In the Gospels, the first words that the Lord Jesus speaks as he begins his public ministry are unmistakably a call to conversion: "This is the time of fulfillment. The kingdom of God is at hand. Repent, and believe in the gospel" (Mk 1:15). There is no avoiding the urgency in his voice, and no getting around that word *repent*. Throughout his public ministry, he calls on everyone with whom he comes in contact to turn away from evil deeds and to accept the Gospel, the new Law of love, into their hearts and into their lives.

As he goes along, the Lord encounters sinners and stretches out his hand to welcome and to heal them. He does not make light of their sins; on the contrary, he often addresses their misdeeds head-on and tells them to "sin no more" (cf. Jn 8:11). At the same time, he tells parables that reveal the extraordinary compassion of God for sinners. Stories like the Good Shepherd who searches for the lost sheep or the woman who sweeps the whole house looking for one lost coin insist that God the Father and the angels in heaven rejoice every time a sinner turns away from evil and back to friendship with God. And the well-loved parable known as the "Prodigal Son" might just as well be called the "Prodigal Father," so abundantly, wastefully generous is the father in the story with his generous love.

Although his younger son treated him as if he were already dead, asking for his inheritance and then throwing it away, when the son finally wises up and returns home, Jesus tells us that "while he was still a long way off, his father caught sight of him" (Lk 15:20) and ran out to meet him. In other words, the father had been waiting and hoping for his son's return the whole time he had been away. As soon as he saw him on the road, he immediately went to him. The son barely had time to get out a tiny bit of his weak, pre-rehearsed attempt at an apology, and the father had already forgiven him, embraced him, and welcomed him back. The parable reinforces what the theological virtue of hope is meant to teach us: that in all things, including forgiveness and conversion, God takes the initiative. He comes to meet us where we are and gives us the grace to do what we are not able to do on our own.

In addition to revealing the Father's abundant mercy by his teaching and parables, the Lord Jesus likewise reveals it in his actions. Numerous stories recount him forgiving people's sins and his interactions with them before and after; these situations often led him into conflict with the religious leaders of his day, who rightly insisted that "God alone can forgive sins" (Mk 2:7)—and then failed to make the connection with the divinity of Christ. He showed compassion to those who had been burdened by sin; often, he stayed and dined with so-called "public sinners" like tax collectors and prostitutes—another habit that did not endear him to the authorities. Many of his healings of sin are connected with miraculous physical healings as well to demonstrate the deep connection between the mystery of sin and the reality of suffering and death in the world—the story of the healing of the paralyzed man who is brought to Jesus by four of his friends and lowered down through a hole in the roof (see Mk 2:1–12) is the most obvious example, and an occasion that Jesus himself used as proof of his divine identity.

Among the many stories of miraculous healings recorded in the synoptic Gospels, there is one that, while it does not explicitly mention Jesus forgiving sins, nevertheless is very helpful for our understanding of how Jesus approaches us when he calls us to be converted. The story stands out for several reasons. The first is that it is one of the few stories that is recorded *only* by Mark and not picked up by Matthew and Luke. An explanation for this might be found in its other distinguishing characteristics: it is intensely, almost uncomfortably, intimate and tactile, even as physical miracles go, and it is the only recorded miracle that Jesus seems to have difficulty carrying out.

The story is recorded in the eighth chapter of the Gospel according to Mark, beginning at verse 22. It takes place in Bethsaida, the hometown of the apostles Peter, Andrew, and Philip (see Jn 1:44). Matthew tells us that this was one of "the towns where most of his mighty deeds had been done" (Mt 11:20) and that Jesus had condemned the inhabitants of Bethsaida for their lack of faith and their refusal to respond to him based on what they had seen him do in their midst.

When Jesus arrives in Bethsaida, some people bring a blind man to him and ask him to heal the man. Because of the general atmosphere of unbelief in the town, before he works the miracle, the first thing that Jesus does is to remove the man from the situation; Mark tells us that Jesus took him by the hand and led him outside the village (see Mk 8:23). Now, the way that we visualize this makes all the difference to the way that we understand the story. I wonder how many people have ever had the experience of leading a person who is blind. The one thing that you cannot do is to literally take a blind person by the hand and pull him along by walking in front of him: it's much too dangerous to move quickly without regarding how the other person is moving behind you. Of course, it is equally unhelpful to stand behind a blind person and push him along with your hand on his back; the only way to lead a blind person is to walk side-by-side, extending your arm so that the blind person can put his arm on yours.

This means that in order to lead him outside the village, the Lord had to adjust his pace to that of the blind man—he couldn't pull him, couldn't drag him, couldn't rush him, but could only move as fast as the blind man was able (and willing) to go. Remember, other people brought the blind man to Jesus—Mark doesn't indicate whether he came willingly or not, whether he was enthusiastic about meeting the traveling preacher that day—and there's nothing in the story to give us any indication that they had ever met before. So, as they were walking along, not only would Jesus have to have been slowing down to the blind man's pace; he would have had to explain to him where they were going; warn him ahead of time of obstacles, twists and turns, and other dangers in their path; and, most importantly, would have had to offer him reassurance about just who he was, that he had his best interests at heart, and that he was trustworthy. I don't know about you, but I would give anything to be able to listen in on that whispered conversation on the road out of Bethsaida.

Once they got outside the village, Jesus set about curing the disease that afflicted the man and kept him isolated from his friends and neighbors. Mark tells us that the healing came through physical contact: the Lord spit into his hands and applied the saliva to the man's eyes. When he asked the man what he could see, he received a response that may confuse us at first; Mark tells us that "looking up he replied, 'I see people looking like trees and walking'" (Mk 8:24). In other words, his sight was partially restored at first, but his vision is still distorted; it is not until Jesus touches his eyes a second time that he is able to see clearly and distinctly (v. 25). At this point, the Lord sends him home, telling him "not even [to] go into the village" (v. 26), the site of so much faithlessness.

What are we to make of this "partial" miracle? We must admit that this two-stage process is unusual; as I suggested a moment ago, it may be a factor in Matthew and Luke's decision not to include this story in their Gospels. Certainly, the answer cannot be that the Lord Jesus was experiencing any kind of limitation in his power to work the miracle. By this time in Mark's Gospel—chapter eight— he has cast out demons; healed the sick, the lame, and the deaf; fed thousands of people; walked on water; and even raised the dead. The crowds that saw him at work proclaimed, "He has done all things well" (Mk 7:37). No, if there is an obstacle to the healing power of Jesus working all at once, or to its full potential, it comes, not from the Lord, but from the recipient of the miracle, from the blind man. He receives the healing in stages because that is the only way that he is able to be healed.

Remember, he has been living in Bethsaida, presumably for some time, perhaps for his whole life, and Bethsaida has rejected the ministry of Jesus so completely that the Lord singles it out for specific condemnation. Before Jesus even begins the miracle, his first move is to take the man out of the town, away from the faithless crowd, away from the obstacles of his environment. Is it so very difficult to imagine, then, that this faithless environment has had an impact on the man who has been living in the midst of it—that the external obstacles have gradually gotten into his mind and heart and become internal obstacles as well? This is a process that does not happen all at once, and so the internal obstacles to receiving the Lord and his gifts are not removed all at once either. Rather, repeated contact with Jesus and his saving touch removes the obstacles and heals the wounds over time.

What gives us hope is the realization in this story that Jesus is patient and understanding as the man goes through this process. It would have been all too easy for him when the man reported his vision of "walking trees" to have rejected him as just one more faithless Bethsaidan among many, obviously unworthy of a miracle because he couldn't put his trust in God. Perhaps we might even expect Jesus to act like this—to tell the blind man, "Come back when you're really ready, when you really mean it"—because we assume that that is the kind of thing he will say to us, and so we keep our distance from him until we feel like we have everything pretty well figured out. But the Lord shows no sign of impatience, makes no rebukes and places no demands on the man who literally doesn't see the whole picture right away. Rather, just as he adjusted his pace to the speed at which the blind man was able to walk with him, Jesus stays with him now and continues to reach out to him for as long as it takes until his healing is complete.

For as long as it takes: this is the real measure of Christ's love for us, and this is what gives us the ability to hope in his mercy and to trust in his love. Of course, the true depth of his mercy is shown to us on the Cross, when he loves us to the end and lays down his life in order to save us and the whole human race from our sins. Writing in his encyclical on hope about the judgment that awaits each of us at the end of our lives, Pope Benedict notes the difference that the Passion of Christ makes to the way we will encounter him. The same difference applies to the encounter with Christ that is part of our ongoing conversion. The pope explains:

> This encounter with him, as it burns us, transforms and frees us, allowing us to become truly ourselves. All that we build during our lives can prove to be mere straw, pure bluster, and it collapses. Yet in the pain of this encounter, when the impurity and sickness of our lives become evident to us, there lies salvation. His gaze, the touch of his heart heals us through an undeniably painful transformation "as through fire". But it is a blessed pain, in which the holy power of his love sears through us like a flame, enabling us to become totally ourselves and thus totally of God.
>
> In this way the inter-relation between justice and grace also becomes clear: the way we live our lives is not immaterial, but our defilement does not stain us forever if we have at least continued to reach out towards Christ, towards truth and towards love. Indeed, it has already been burned away through Christ's Passion. At the moment of judgment we

experience and we absorb the overwhelming power of his love over all the evil in the world and in ourselves. The pain of love becomes our salvation and our joy.[5]

In the next section, we're going to take an in-depth look at the life of someone who had a very personal, and rather painful, encounter with the Lord that burned and transformed him and did, at the end, truly set him free. We can learn from his experience, and from his very honest account of his own state of mind and heart, to hope in the Lord should we find ourselves in a similar situation.

Breaking Free From Sin—Saint Augustine

Previously, we examined the importance of the virtue of hope in the essential Christian task of conversion, the lifelong process of turning away from sin and selfishness and turning toward God and the friendship for which he has created us. No discussion of conversion would be complete without discussing the person who is arguably the Church's most famous convert, at least if sales of his spiritual autobiography are any indication. I'm speaking, of course, about Saint Augustine, whose *Confessions* has been a best seller since its appearance in the late fourth century, and continues to inspire and instruct us today.

The *Confessions of Saint Augustine* is written as a dialogue between the saint and God as Augustine looks back over his life to acknowledge and give thanks for the many interventions of Divine Providence that he can see only

---

[5]   Benedict XVI, *Spe Salvi*, 47.

in retrospect. The blessing for which he is most grateful throughout the book is his memory, which allows him to analyze his emotions, his prayers, even his temptations at various stages of his life. As we shall see, Augustine was a complicated man, and not an automatic saint. He also has a gift for candor, honesty with himself and with God, that grants us the privilege some eighteen centuries later to benefit from the spiritual and psychological insights that he acquired through difficult, often painful experience.

Augustine was born at Tagaste, now the village of Souk Ahras in northeast Algeria, on November 13, 354. His mother, Monica, was Christian, but his father, Patricius, was pagan. Although Patricius, a Roman citizen, would eventually accept the faith, when Augustine and his brother were young, their father was not yet enthusiastic about their mother raising the children as Christians. Augustine was enrolled as a *catechumen*—a candidate for religious instruction and eventual baptism—but his connection with the Church was minimal in his early years.

What his father was concerned about was that Augustine should receive a top-notch education. Augustine was extraordinarily bright, and his parents and their friends were well-off enough to be able to nurture his intellectual gifts by sending him to school, first in Madaurus and then in the capital city of Carthage. Augustine took up the study of *rhetoric*, the ancient art of public speaking and persuasion that was such an important part of community and civic life in the Roman Empire. Part politics, part communications, part public relations, a career in rhetoric would mean that Augustine would become well-known and, if he were good at his work, would have influence and be in demand among very influential people in society. As it turned out, Augustine was very good at rhetoric.

Around this time, though, Augustine was also discovering how enjoyable it could be to be very bad. As he looks back at his life, he admits that he had been "a wretched boy"[6] more concerned with pleasing his peers than with doing what was pleasing to God. He repeatedly told lies; he sneaked around to watch lewd shows at music halls; he stole from his parents' pantry, either for himself or to bribe his friends; he cheated at games.[7] As he grew older, the catalog of his sins grew with him. In his teenage years, he became preoccupied with sins of the flesh: "What was it that delighted me?" he asks. "Only loving and being loved."[8] By the age of sixteen, he had lost his virginity and begun a sexual relationship with a young woman; when his parents found out about this, they brought him home from school to live with them.

Augustine's mother pleaded with him to stop what he was doing, to follow the Lord and his commandments, and to change his ways. Sadly, Augustine dismissed her entreaties; filled as he was with pride and defensiveness, he writes that "these warnings seemed to me mere woman's talk, which I would have blushed to heed."[9] Instead, now that he was home and among his friends from childhood,

---

6   Augustine, *Confessions* I.30, trans. Maria Boulding (Hyde Park, NY: New City Press, 1997), 59.

7   Ibid.

8   *Confessions* II.2, 62.

9   *Confessions* II.7, 66.

his debaucheries grew worse, because he felt the need to keep up with the crowd. The more that his friends talked about their exploits, the more Augustine felt pressured to have something to talk about, and if he didn't have a story to tell, he would make something up so as not to feel left out. As his behavior got worse and worse, he describes "a dark fog [that] cut [him] off from [the] bright truth" that comes from God.[10]

As devastating as Augustine's lustful behavior was to his mother, Monica—and as bad as it rightly seems to us—there is one more incident from his teenage years that Augustine looks back on as even worse. His family had a vineyard, he relates, and close by it a neighbor had an orchard that contained a pear tree. On a certain night, Augustine and his friends stayed up late after dark, playing games and carrying on, waiting for the right opportunity in the dead of night to go and rob that pear tree and carry off its abundant fruit. But here's the thing about that incident: Augustine didn't want to eat the pears, and neither did his friends. The pears on that tree were ugly and didn't taste particularly good. They ate a few and threw the rest to the pigs. Their motive in stealing was not for personal gain, or even for any particular pleasure: "There was no motive for my malice except malice,"[11] Augustine was forced to admit, and it horrified him.

Looking back, Augustine realizes a couple of important things about the sins of his youth—which can be important lessons for us as well. The first we have alluded to

---

[10]   *Confessions* II.8, 67.
[11]   *Confessions* II.9, 68.

already: the influence of peer pressure. Why did he steal those pears? Why did he lie and cheat and steal? Why did he go to such extremes of debauchery and lust? Augustine was always free, and always had the ability to make his own choices and to say no, but at least in part he felt driven on, time and again, by his friends. He didn't like it, not at the time, not looking back, but it was true. "What an exceedingly unfriendly form of friendship that was!" he exclaims to God in retrospect. "Let the others only say, 'Come on, let's go and do it!' and I am ashamed to hold back from the shameless act."[12]

There is something else at work in Augustine's heart and mind during this time that keeps him enslaved to his passions and leads him to sin. In later years, Augustine came to realize that when he was sinning, he was looking in the wrong place for something that he needed; that, in a sense, he was seeking God but not knowing where to find him. "In vice," he writes, "there lurks a counterfeit beauty"[13]—pride and ambition, curiosity and sloth, even lust, Augustine insists, come about when we pursue qualities that are good *when they belong to God and come from God* (like power, honor, knowledge, rest, and love), and instead seek them for ourselves and on our own terms. "In this lay my sin," he explains, "that not in [God] was I seeking pleasures, distinctions and truth, but in myself and the rest of his creatures, and so I fell headlong into pains, confusions and errors."[14]

---

12   *Confessions* II.17, 73.

13   *Confessions* II.13, 70.

14   *Confessions* I.31, 61.

In 371, Augustine went to Carthage to continue his training in rhetoric; his behavior did not improve. On the contrary, it was here that he began a thirteen-year affair with a woman whom he would often refer to as "The One" and with whom he would have a son, whom he named Adeodatus, "God-given." After completing his studies, Augustine returned to Tagaste to teach for a couple of years and then came back to Carthage to open a school of rhetoric, which he led for nine years. In 383, he moved to Rome, where he hoped to be able to make an impact among the "best and brightest" rhetoricians and politicians in the empire. His reputation preceded him, and he was able to pick and choose his students from among the wealthy and important families. However, he soon found most of his students to be apathetic and uncooperative, and when the time came round for them to pay their tuition, they disappeared. Disillusioned with life in the city, Augustine applied for a position as professor of rhetoric for the imperial court at Milan, about three hundred miles north of Rome.

Augustine arrived in Milan in late 384. Shortly after he arrived there, he met the bishop of the city, Ambrose, who was Augustine's equal in terms of intellectual ability and rhetorical gifts but possessed an abundance of one quality that Augustine seemed to lack: compassion. Augustine relates that when he first came to Milan, he was immediately drawn in by Ambrose simply because the bishop was kind to him. He could see that he practiced the kind of Christian charity that he was preaching, and although Augustine was not yet ready to listen to, much less accept, the Gospel message, his early encounters with the bishop laid the foundations for what would happen later.

In Milan, Augustine was undergoing a period of soul-searching and inner turmoil. In Carthage and Rome, he had been an adherent of a philosophy called Manicheanism, which was based on the notion of a fundamental *dualism* in the universe: a good God created spiritual things good, including the soul, and an evil god or spirit created material things evil, including the visible world and the human body. This "soul good, body bad" mentality led to two kinds of Manichees: the very serious initiates, who were celibate, fasted on water and vegetables, and lived a very ascetical life to avoid the evils of the body; and the much less strict crowds, who, because the body was essentially evil and passing away, could eat, drink, and be merry in the body because it didn't really matter anyway. Ultimately, this philosophy was unsatisfying, intellectually and morally, for Augustine. He was looking for an alternative but was not quite sure where to go. He was not quite sure that he was ready for a complete break with the past, either; his prayer was often, "Grant me chastity and self-control, but please not yet."[15]

In the midst of this inner conflict, Augustine did what he usually did: he surrounded himself with his friends and leaned on them for support. He never had much problem making friends, and in Milan, it was no different. They had use of a villa at Cassiciacum, just outside the city, and it was there, in the summer of 386, that Augustine would

---

[15]   *Confessions* VIII.17, 198.

form the definitive friendship that would give purpose and meaning to his whole life.

The difficulty for Augustine as he was struggling to understand his own mind was that his friends seemed to be losing theirs. Little by little, Augustine had been feeling that he should do something with his life. Then one day an old acquaintance named Placianus came to visit Augustine at Cassiciacum. Placianus had recently read the *Life of Saint Anthony the Great*, a biography of the first monk to go out into the deep desert of Egypt to live as a hermit. This book, just recently published by St. Athanasius, had affected him and his friends so profoundly, Placianus explained, that they had decided to leave their training and worldly careers—even their fiancées—behind, to give their money to the poor, and to dedicate themselves to serving God and the Church. Augustine was at once impressed with their resolve and dedication and ashamed with himself for not being able to make anything like a similar commitment.

This inner conflict escalated into a violent crisis, a "quarrel with [his] soul" over his future and the meaning of his life.[16] Augustine rushed to see his friend Alypius, who was staying with him at the villa, and begged him for answers; then he ran off into the garden to try to work things out for himself. When Alypius followed behind his friend, he found Augustine in a pitiful state: pacing back and forth, tearing at his hair, his cheeks were flushed, and he was on the verge of tears, groaning from the depths of his heart.

---

[16] *Confessions* VIII.19, 199.

This outward display was mild compared to the turmoil going on inside Augustine: "All I knew was that I was going mad," he writes, "aware of the evil that I was but unaware of the good I was soon to become. . . . I was shaken by violent anger because I could form no resolve to enter into a covenant with you, though in my bones I knew that this was what I ought to do, and everything in me lauded such a course to the skies."[17]

Looking back on this moment, Augustine marveled at how much activity he was able to carry out, though he was unable to do the one thing he needed most to do—that one act of the will that would have moved him away from sin and toward God. His heart and body were extremely active, but his will, in this respect, was paralyzed. He asks himself what could possibly have held him back from making this move when intellectually he knew it was so good and practically it would have been so simple to do. The answer he arrived at should not surprise us, knowing as we do not only where Augustine has been but what we ourselves experience. "This partial willing and partial non-willing is not so bizarre," he says, "but [is] a sickness of the mind, which cannot rise with its whole self on the wings of truth because it is heavily burdened by habit."[18] What Augustine needs to do, and what at least part of him really wishes to do, is to make an act of virtue—which is a good habit that tends toward the ultimate good, God. But first he must find a way to overcome the cumulative power

---

[17]   *Confessions* VIII.19, 200.

[18]   *Confessions* VIII.21, 201.

of years of practicing bad habits that have been tending in the opposite direction—the very real power of vice.

Augustine began to realize what was holding him, and he began to try to break free. Back and forth he argued with himself about whether he was really ready to give up his old ways—he describes them as long-time friends and remembers almost hearing them speaking to him in those difficult moments, grabbing him by the cloak "and murmuring in my ear, 'Do you mean to get rid of us? Shall we never be your companions again after that moment . . . never . . . never again? From that time onward so-and-so will be forbidden to you, all your life long.'"[19] This was the worst part of it, he recalls, the hints and the insinuations that he would not be able to live without the things he had become accustomed to for so long. It was becoming dangerous for Augustine in these moments, and then, at last, God intervened.

In his mind's eye, Augustine thought he could behold a vision, sent to him "from that country toward which I was facing"—the figure of Chastity, surrounded by a multitude of joyful, chaste young people, calling out to him to throw himself on the Lord's mercy and put his old life behind him.[20] Augustine broke down in tears and wept for a long time because he still did not know if he had the strength to do what he ought to do. Finally, he cried out to the Lord, "I uttered cries of misery: 'Why must I go on

---

19   *Confessions* VIII.26, 204.
20   *Confessions* VIII.27, 205.

saying, "Tomorrow . . . tomorrow"? Why not now? Why not put an end to my depravity this very hour?'"[21]

Suddenly, Augustine heard a child's voice coming from the other side of the garden wall, singing a curious phrase repeatedly: *"Pick it up and read, pick it up and read."* He couldn't think of any children's game that included this line as part of it, so it dawned on him that this must be a revelation from God meant for him. His eyes fixed on the Bible which lay on a table in the garden; he picked it up, opened it without deliberately choosing a specific page, and determined to read the first passage on which his eyes fell as addressed to him directly by God. This is what he read, from the letter of Saint Paul to the Romans: "Let us conduct ourselves properly as in the day, not in orgies and drunkenness, not in promiscuity and licentiousness, not in rivalry and jealousy. But put on the Lord Jesus Christ, and make no provision for the desires of the flesh" (Rom 13:13–14).

By the time Augustine had reached the end of the verse, he says, he was convinced: all of his doubts had gone, all of his hesitating was over, and he was ready to give himself over to Christ. He went inside to share the good news with his mother, and soon sought out Ambrose for instruction in the faith; by Easter 387, he was baptized. He returned to Africa the following year, and was ordained a priest in 391 in Hippo Regius, now Annaba, Algeria. Four years later, he became bishop of Hippo and served in that role until his death in 430 at the age of seventy-five. He was known as an exemplary priest and bishop, and a

---

[21]   *Confessions* VIII.28, 206.

fantastic preacher; his skill at philosophy and theology, and his ability to defend the Faith against misunderstandings, have earned him the traditional title of Doctor of the Church.

There is no doubt that this change in Augustine's life was sudden and extreme—even he would agree that to say that it was like "night and day" seems a bit of an understatement. So how did it come about, and what does it have to do with the theological virtue of hope? Well, we have taken a lot of time to dissect Augustine's state of mind, and I think one thing is abundantly clear: there is just no way that he was going to make this decision on his own. If it were up to him to decide—to finally make that one act of the will all on his own that was going to be the definitive break between the old Augustine and the new— then he would still be in the garden in Cassiciacum today trying to make up his mind.

Instead, the Lord intervenes to help Augustine when he needs it the most. This is not a violation of his free will: remember, Augustine cried out in the garden for help, and God was merely responding to this cry and giving Augustine the grace to do what he was not able to do on his own. Like the father in the story of the prodigal son, the Lord is waiting for Augustine to make even the smallest move toward him, just the tiniest movement of repentance that he is able, and then he rushes out to him to bring him along the rest of the way, giving him reassurance and inspiration to resolve all of his doubts and to assist the necessary act of the will that leads to his complete conversion.

This is the underlying theological principle of the virtue

of hope—that we not only press on toward our goal but that we rely on the grace and strength that comes from God in order to be able to attain it. Augustine was agitated in the garden because he could *see* intellectually where he ought to have been, but he could not get there with his will; in fact, in the *Confessions* he describes his conversion as both the shortest and the longest journey he ever had to make. Once he was able to cry out for help—with just the tiniest bit of theological hope, itself a gift from God—he received the grace that he needed to make that journey successfully.

What was that grace, exactly? For Augustine, it came in the form of revelations—spiritual understandings about the moral life and where he ought to be situated in relationship to Christ. We have seen that he had a kind of vision of Chastity, who invited him to throw his cares on the Lord; in fact, the vision spoke to him in words that were very personal and just what Augustine needed to hear: "Why try to stand by yourself, only to lose your footing? Cast yourself on [the Lord] and do not be afraid: he will not step back and let you fall. Cast yourself upon him trustfully; he will support and heal you."[22] All his life, Augustine had done most of his evil deeds, at least in part, because he was afraid of being alone, because he did not want to be left out of the crowd. Chastity addresses this fear and assures him that virtue will lead to real friendship with Christ. She offers him real hope, which takes the things of this world—things that we thought we should rely on—and places them in their proper context

---

[22]   *Confessions* VIII.27, 205.

in relation to our true happiness: communion with God in the kingdom of heaven.

When Augustine was able to see clearly that his real happiness would come from heaven and that this would be enough for him—that his real and best friend would be Christ Jesus and that the Lord would support him in every difficulty, that the fact that he had lived one way for so long did not *have to* hold him back from living differently if he had the hope to change—then at last he was able to hand himself over and be converted. He experienced this turning point in his life as a "returning point," a sort of homecoming to where he should have been all along: "Late have I loved you, Beauty so ancient and so new, late have I loved you! Lo, you were within, but I outside, seeking there for you . . . you were with me, but I was not with you. You called, shouted, broke through my deafness; you flared, blazed, banished my blindness; you lavished your fragrance, I gasped, and now I pant for you; I tasted you, and I hunger and thirst; you touched me, and I burned for your peace.[23]

A theologian and pastor once advised his flock to "sin boldly" so as to be able to experience God's mercy to the full extent that Augustine, for example, had it lavished upon him. I would not recommend this; it is far better to stay near the Lord as much as possible. Still, we can learn many lessons from Saint Augustine's experiences without having to go through all of them ourselves. In the next section, we will take a closer look at some of these lessons

---

[23]   *Confessions* X.38, 262.

as we learn to hold fast to hope through the lifelong process of conversion.

Persevering in Holiness—Venerable Matt Talbot

When we were considering the story of Saint Augustine, one of the things that stood out about his description of his passions and his temptations was his realization that he was always seeking counterfeits of beauty. He did prideful things rather than seek a real relationship with God; he went after ambition rather than try to be known for doing good. From the very beginning, he seemed to recognize all of his lustful exploits as a misplaced chasing after a loving relationship that could really satisfy. When, finally, he was able, with the help of divine grace, to hand himself over to God, he began to see things clearly—both the counterfeits that he had been chasing and the realities he had wanted all along. The comparison stunned him and led him to the prayer of praise which began with his lament that he had started loving God so late.

The challenging thing about conversion—real conversion, not just talking about it—is just this moment of revelation when we begin to see things as they really are. Of course, to see the realities that God is offering us is, or will be, beautiful, uplifting, joyful. But at the same time, we will be confronted with the fact that we may have been chasing falsehoods—that we may have been kidding ourselves for a while. Or, worse, we may have known all along that what we were choosing was less than real, and now, for the first time, we may be forced to admit it to ourselves and to God. Anticipation of this aspect of conversion, this humble honest moment of self-awareness and admission, is sometimes enough to scare us off.

Theological hope comes to our aid in moments like these, with the reassurance that the truth is never something to fear. The virtue of hope, as we have already seen many times, is given to us for the very purpose of helping us to see and prioritize correctly—to place the things of this world in their proper place in relation to eternal life. The more we hope, the clearer our vision, and because we do not hope alone, but always with God to help us, we need never be afraid of what we shall see, because he will be there to guide and assist us. We may not be pleased with what meets our eye, but he will always provide us with the grace to handle it.

Mathew Talbot was born on May 2, 1856, on Aldboro Court in Dublin, the second of twelve children and one of eight brothers. His family was extremely poor—like most of the Irish in those post-famine days—and although Matt was able to attend Christian Brothers schools for a year or so, his formal education quickly came to an end. He left school at the age of twelve and took a job as a messenger boy for Edward and John Burke, wine merchants who bottled stout for Guinness and Youngers.

Within the year, Matt came home from work one evening drunk on Guinness. His father was furious; he gave him a severe beating, made him quit his job, and found him a new one working for the local authority overseeing ports and docks. This made the situation even worse: Matt was sent to run messages to the "bonded stores" where whiskey was sold; a friendly dram from the shopkeeper to the boy from the Port and Docks Board ensured that soon, at the age of twelve, Matt Talbot had become an alcoholic.

For the next sixteen years, Matt's life was deeply affected by his addiction, although he found ways to cope with it at work. When he was seventeen, he became a bricklayer with a contracting firm called Pemberton's; he was an excellent laborer and was never late, and was often held up as an example for his fellows to imitate. When the whistle blew at the end of the day, however, he and his coworkers could spend all evening at the local pub, drinking away all the money he had earned by his hard work. Often enough, he would take his eighteen shillings directly from the paymaster to the publican on Saturday afternoon to pay his tab in advance; by Tuesday, the money would be all gone—all drunk, more like it—and he would pawn his boots to buy just another round or two and walk home in his socks.

One Saturday afternoon, when Matt was twenty-eight years old, would change his life forever. That particular Saturday was not a pay day; Matt had been too drunk the previous week to report to work at all, so there were no wages to collect that day. Now he was sober and thirsty, but had not a penny with which to buy a drink. He was sure, though, that the many friends and coworkers for whom he had bought so many rounds over the years would come to his aid in his hour of need. Matt and his brother stood near O'Meara's Pub on a spot where he knew he would cross paths with many of his coworkers coming along from Pemberton's after work. The men who he had thought were his friends came by in groups of twos and threes;

Matt waited for them to invite him along with them, but they did not even greet him. They simply kept walking as if they could not see him at all. "Matt said later that he was 'cut to the heart' by this treatment and went home."[24]

Matt's mother was surprised to see him home in the middle of the day and in his condition, and she said so: "Matt, you're home early, and you're sober!" After sharing the midday meal with his family, he announced to his mother that he was going to church and was going to take "the pledge"—to promise to abstain from alcohol as a personal sacrifice, as a means of giving good example to others, and in reparation for his past sins of intemperance. He went to the chapel at Holy Cross College, the archdiocesan seminary not far from his house, and, as he related the story, first went to confession and then took the pledge from Father Keane. He initially promised to abstain from alcohol for three months.

In the early days, Matt faced great personal temptations, the power of physical addiction and the pull of memory and habit. More than that, none of his family and friends had taken the pledge with him. So he needed to find some safe place where he could give himself a chance to live the pledge he had made—and he only knew one place where he could be sure his old drinking companions wouldn't come looking for him. He began to attend Mass daily before work and to spend his evenings after work kneeling in a dark corner of a parish church far from the neighborhood where he lived—where he was sure no one would find

---

24   Mary Gaffney, "Matt Talbot—The Workers' Saint," *Reality,* July/August 1999.

him. He described these days as a period of making "new friends"—Jesus, Our Lady, and the saints—and he relied on them to help him to make this change in his life permanent. He was often convinced that he wouldn't be able to follow through on his pledge and prayed fervently to God, "Please, don't let me go back to my old ways. Have mercy on me."[25] After he successfully kept his pledge for three months, he renewed it several times, and then pledged to abstain for the rest of his life. And he managed to keep it, for forty-one years, until his death from heart disease on June 7, 1925, at the age of sixty-nine.

What lessons does Matt Talbot have to teach us about hope and conversion? I think the first insight comes from understanding what it was that caused him to make a change in his life. When we were considering the early life of Saint Augustine, one of things that we learned about his "wild child" ways was that he was heavily influenced, as Augustine himself admits, by the company he was keeping. Time and again Augustine did the things he did because of the pressure he felt to keep up with the crowd—to fit in, to be popular, to be just as bad as everyone else. There was something similar happening in the life of Matt Talbot: he was, on most occasions, the life of the party and spent his money freely to buy drinks for his coworkers, thinking that their companionship meant something to them as well as to him. Once he was penniless and had to depend on them for a change, he realized

---

[25]   Ann Bottenhorn, "'I Ask Only Three Things . . .': The Life of Matt Talbot," *The Word Among Us*, January 2005.

how they truly saw him and found himself isolated and alone.

Yet, rather than plunge deeper into despair as a result of this experience—this being "cut to the heart"—Matt responded by opening himself up to the possibility of conversion, at a tremendous price to himself not only spiritually but emotionally and even physically. Why? Perhaps in those lonely moments on the street corner outside O'Meara's, he came to realize that he was truly not alone. Perhaps he saw, for the very first time, the truth of what Pope Benedict teaches in his encyclical on hope: "When no one listens to me anymore, God still listens to me. When I can no longer talk to anyone or call upon anyone, I can always talk to God. When there is no longer anyone to help me deal with a need or expectation that goes beyond the human capacity for hope, he can help me. When I have been plunged into complete solitude . . . if I pray I am never totally alone."[26]

Surely this was the answer for Matt Talbot, this recognition that God was with him and would continue to be with him to help him to carry out the changes he intended to make in his life. How else can we explain the instantaneous adjustments in his daily schedule, which he seemed to make almost by instinct? He *knew* where he needed to be because he *knew* that he needed to be with God. He knew above all that, especially in the early days of his pledge, in the most difficult moments when it would have been easiest to go back to old habits, he shouldn't be alone. And so he just sat in church in the presence of the

---

[26]   Benedict XVI, *Spe Salvi*, 32.

Blessed Sacrament, where he knew he was safe, because he was with God, the source of his hope. Someone asked him once what he did in there all that time, what he prayed about. His answer was simple: "Oh, I just look at Him, and He looks at me."

Another important lesson from Matt Talbot's life is the way in which he approached "the pledge." It would have been dramatic, even heroic, to have walked into church that day and asked Father Keane to administer the lifelong pledge on the spot. But by this time, Matt had been an alcoholic for sixteen years, since the time he was twelve. He hadn't acquired his addiction overnight, and he knew enough about himself to know that, no matter how strong the call to conversion he was feeling, he wasn't going to shake off old ways of thinking and acting in a day. Instead, he took the pledge for three months—even this temporary pledge he wasn't quite sure he would be able to keep— and renewed it again for a year before committing to it on a perpetual basis. Like the blind man in Mark's Gospel, who received his sight gradually, Matt took on this newfound freedom and commitment in the amount he was able to bear with God's help. There's no sign that God (or Matt) considered this a less-than-worthy commitment. On the contrary, the Lord seems to have rewarded Matt all the more for his humility in not trying to take on too much all at once and gave him the grace to persevere.

So far, the stories we've been considering have all ended with conversions that have been fairly dramatic: a person hears the voice of God calling him to turn away from sin, and, after some initial struggle, the moment of decision

comes and the change is made. After that, with few excep-
tions, there's been very little looking back, not much in
the way of relapses. But sin and addiction are not always
so easily overcome, even with God's grace at work. What
do we do when change comes more slowly? When we are
tempted to fall back to old ways of acting? How long can
we hope that God will remain patient with us?

The classic collection of spiritual stories and sayings
known as the *Evergetinos* was compiled and edited by
Saint Nicodemus of Mount Athos and first published in
1783. In its two hundred chapters, usually published in
four large books, the *Evergetinos* covers a broad range of
topics having to do with the spiritual life in general and the
specific way of life of the Desert Fathers and Mothers, the
monks and nuns who lived in the wildernesses of Egypt,
Syria, and Palestine in the fourth and fifth centuries.

The first five chapters of the *Evergetinos* deal with
repentance, and the very first chapter bears the charming
and reassuring title—really the statement—that "No one
should despair ever, even if he has committed many sins,
but should have hope that through repentance, he shall be
saved."[27] A number of teachings and anecdotes are col-
lected in this first chapter to convince us that this statement is true and to give us the courage to live by it.

Perhaps the most reassuring is a story told by the Desert
Father Saint Amphilóchios. There was a brother—a monk
in the community—he explains, who committed a grave

---

[27]   *The Evergetinos: A Complete Text. Volume I of the First Book.*
        Translated and edited by Bishop Chrysostomos, et al. (Etna,
        CA: Center for Traditional Orthodox Studies, 1988), 17.

sin every day. The word that Amphilóchios uses in Greek to describe this sin lets us know that it was a sexual sin, probably a solitary one. He was overcome by his passions, the saint tells us, and enslaved by this sin—but all was not lost. Each time he sinned, the brother would turn to the Lord with repentance and ask for forgiveness, often with weeping. He would go to the church, kneel before an image of the Lord Jesus, and pray with terribly poignant words:

> Lord, have mercy upon me and take away from me this fearful temptation, for it troubles me fiercely and wounds me with the bitter taste of the pleasures. O my Master, cleanse my person once more, that I may gaze upon Thine Icon and see Thy holy form and the sight of Thy face, brighter than the sun, that my heart might be sweetened and thankful. . . .
>
> My Lord, I swear to Thee on my word, that I shall no longer commit this sin. Only forgive me, Good and Most Merciful Lord, whatever sins I have committed, from the beginning to this moment."[28]

And every time—every single time, Amphilóchios assures us—the brother would receive forgiveness for his sins. Already this may seem a bit difficult for us to believe; sometimes people tend to judge sexual sins more harshly than other sins. What makes it even more difficult to accept this kind of endless mercy is that Amphilóchios tells us that as soon as the man repented, sometimes

---

[28]   Ibid., 28.

as soon as he was out the door of the church, he would fall victim to the same habits and the same temptations. His sinful habits had such a hold on him that over and over again he kept giving in to them, no matter how many times he promised the Lord he was really going to change. Amphilóchios relates that the situation went on this way "for more than ten years."[29]

Lest we begin to focus too much on the faltering of the brother, and his persistent bad habits, Amphilóchios redirects our attention at this point in the story to what is really marvelous: the boundless mercy of God in the face of the brother's repeated sin. While we might look at the persistent sins of the brother, God was on the look-out for his persistent returning and words of repentance, and every time that the brother professed his sorrow, God was ready to accept it. Not once in the story is there any indication that God gave the brother an ultimatum, that he drew a line that said, "I will accept you this many times, but no more." From God, there was only mercy without measure, patience without counting, forgiveness without limits . . . and the same boundless mercy that God showed to the brother is the mercy that he offers to us. This is the reason that we can be hopeful even of overcoming sinful habits.

Amphilóchios tells us that one day when the brother had sinned yet again, and gone yet again to church to repent and to ask forgiveness, the devil himself, fed up with what he considered an unfair situation, appeared in the church to plead his case. God was not just, he complained—the

29   Ibid., 29.

brother clearly mocked God by insincere repentance if he was asking for forgiveness one minute and then going out to sin again the next. Why didn't God strike the brother down, he asked, rather than tolerate and forgive him when he knew full well that he would simply go out and sin again? After all, Satan had been cast out of heaven for one transgression, but this brother, who sinned repeatedly and often, received mercy over and over, though he clearly did not deserve it or appreciate it.

At this point, a voice is heard from the sanctuary; it is the Lord answering the charge that Satan has made. Far from being unfair, the Lord insists, he is being perfectly consistent. Indeed, by forgiving the brother, he is doing what he once commanded Peter and the apostles that they must do for their brothers: "I, who am merciful and love mankind, who counseled my laudable Apostle, Peter, to forgive sins seven times seventy (Mt 18:22), do I not show him mercy and compassion? Indeed, simply because he flees to me, I will not turn him away until I have won him over. . . . I neither turn away nor reject anyone, even if he should fall many times a day and many times return to me."[30]

Is it possible for us truly to hope in the Lord to this extent, to believe that his mercy is really this generous, this limitless? Part of the reason that God infuses the theological virtue of hope into us is precisely for this purpose: to make it possible for us to trust him like this. For to do so is simply to take him at his word, to believe him when he tells us who he is and what he is going to do. As surely as it is a tendency of our fallen human nature to sin, it is

---

[30] Ibid., 30–31.

part of the very nature of our good and merciful God to look with pity on those who turn to him—as the Psalmist says, "Merciful and gracious is the LORD, slow to anger, abounding in mercy" (Ps 103:8).

Sometimes the fact that we fall repeatedly—and therefore that we have to continue to turn to the Lord and to hope in his mercy—is the best and most effective way for us to learn that the source of our strength and conversion is God and not ourselves. Moses of Sketis, known as Moses the Ethiopian, is one of the shining lights among the desert monks of the fourth century—but he went into the desert originally fleeing from the police. He had been the head of a band of thieves, a highway robber and a sheep rustler to boot, and on at least one occasion had attempted murder, seeking vengeance on a shepherd whose dog had sounded the alarm on one of his burglaries. Hiding out among the caves, he met the monks of the desert monastery at Sketis, spiritual sons of Saint Anthony the Great, and was encouraged by them to shape up his life.

He eventually did have a change of heart and began to follow the monastic rule of prayer and penance. He had brought his memory of past sins and his collection of grudges and bad habits along with him, though, so he found it very difficult at first to achieve peace of mind in the solitude of the wilderness. For several years, he thought that the way to do it would be to take on extra, secret penances at night, and so he deprived himself of sleep, walked long distances to get water for the older monks, and did various other tasks that did little but wear him out and make him physically ill.

Early one morning, his spiritual father, Abba Isidore, came to get Moses and took him up a hillside to have him watch the sun rise. He explained that just as the sky gets lighter little by little as the sun comes up slowly, so we have to make progress in holiness gradually as the light of Christ shines brighter in us and overcomes our bad habits. Moses protested and said he would not give up on his hard penances until all of his temptations were gone—otherwise, he was sure he would have no peace. At last, Abba Isidore had him kneel and placed his hands on his head; all at once, the temptations were completely gone, and Moses felt calm for the first time in years. When Abba Isidore told him that the temptations would never, ever return, Moses was even happier. However, he told him, "Do not boast within yourself and say, 'I have overcome the demons,'"[31] for God had taken them away on his own initiative.

Ultimately, as we have seen through the stories of all of these "heroes of hope," it is God who accomplishes every good work, especially when it comes to rooting out selfishness and sin from our lives. Our one task is to hope in him—to open our hearts trustingly to receive his grace, which enables us to turn away from sin and to turn toward the life he has won for us. Yet conversion is but the first step on our journey toward the goal; we are definitely still "on the way." Next, we will consider how hope allows us to respond generously to our vocation: to give freely of ourselves and to cooperate in the saving mission of Christ.

---

[31] *The Life of Our Holy Father Among the Saints Moses the Ethiopian* (Seattle: St. Nectarios Press, 1991), 6.

3

We Dare to Serve the Lord

Discerning the Lord's Plan—The Holy Family

In the last chapter, we were looking at how the theological virtue of hope strengthens and encourages us on our journey toward heaven by helping us in the lifelong process of conversion. This work of gradually, persistently turning away from sin and turning toward God reorients our lives toward our ultimate happiness: the friendship with God for which we were created. The virtue of hope trains us to keep our hearts and minds fixed on what's really important so that we can see ourselves as God sees us and make the necessary changes in our lives patiently and honestly. Hope, because it is the particular virtue of people who are "on the way" to their ultimate goal, not only marks out the path for us but keeps us mindful that there is still time to follow it so that we can dedicate ourselves to the work of conversion without becoming discouraged.

Now we are going to take a look at how each of us is moving toward deeper friendship with God, and toward our ultimate destiny, along a particular path which God has chosen for us—what we call our *vocation*. We have already discussed this concept in terms of the overarching vocation or call to beatitude that belongs to each of us by virtue of our being created in the image and likeness of God. We are made for relationships and called to make a gift of ourselves to others—we are created and destined to love as God loves. Within this fundamental human vocation, though, each of us finds a more specific way of serving the Lord and of participating in the work of building up his kingdom.

This particular mode of service takes the form of what is usually called a *state in life*—one of several ways of living in the Church that is characterized by a particular form of commitment, an intentional gift of self, and usually by a type of consecration. There are, by tradition, four states of life:

- the *ordained ministry*—bishops, priests, and deacons, who make a gift of themselves to the whole Church in the role of servant leaders, acting in the person of Christ to celebrate the sacraments, to shepherd and teach the faithful. They are set apart for this ministry by the sacrament of Holy Orders, which hands on the sacred authority given to the apostles by the Lord Jesus, and transmitted by them to their successors by prayer and the laying on of hands.
- the *consecrated life*—monks, nuns, and Religious men and women who live in community

life, who make gifts of themselves to the Church as radical examples of living the evangelical counsels of poverty, chastity, and obedience, and of the importance of fraternal charity. They are consecrated by the vows or promises they freely make by which they bind themselves to Christ and to one another, and to observe the evangelical counsels for their whole lives.

- *married people*, who make a total gift of self to one another and so become a living sign to the world of the permanent, faithful, life-giving bond between Christ and the Church. They are consecrated by the free gift of their whole lives to one another which they make in the sacrament of Matrimony.

- *committed single people*, who have determined to remain in the single lay state and make a gift of self to their family, their church, and their community in generous service. Although there is not a specific rite of consecration for such people (perhaps there should be!), they receive grace for their vocation from the Lord in their daily life of prayer and participation in the sacraments.

As we can see, there is a great diversity in these four basic states in life, and within each broad category are almost limitless ways to live them out. This variety is important and enriching to the life of the Church and does not imply that one person's contribution is greater or lesser than another's. On the contrary, all of the vocations work together for the good of the whole Church, as the *Catechism* points out: "In virtue of their rebirth in Christ there exists among all the Christian faithful a true equality with regard to dignity and the activity whereby all cooperate in the building up of the Body of Christ in accord with each one's own condition and function."[1]

The key, according to the *Catechism*, is for each person to find the vocation and the state in life which is "proper to each one"[2] and which corresponds to the diversity of gifts which God bestows on his children. Coming to understand our vocation is a process, called *discernment*, and it isn't always easy. Time, distractions, confusion, mixed messages, temptations—these and many other factors can work against us as we try to understand where God is leading us. As you may already have guessed, in the process of discernment, the virtue of hope is an indispensable help.

Classical spiritual theology suggested that the thoughts that come into the mind and heart originate from several sources—from the world, in the form of distractions; from the Evil One, in the form of temptations; from the self, in the form of desires and appetites; or from God, in the form of inspirations. Discernment means learning, through experience and right judgment, to consider carefully each thought that occurs to the mind and heart and to be able to determine correctly its true source. Once this is done, we can make a correct judgment whether to reject the thought, to ignore it, or to follow it. Applying this idea to our vocation means that we listen carefully for the voice

---

[1]   *Catechism of the Catholic Church*, 872.

[2]   Ibid., 871.

of God, as he makes his will known in prayer, in his Word, in the suggestions of others, and in the circumstances of our daily lives. Once we come to know what he sounds like, we can hear what he is saying and then follow him with confidence.

Of course, all of this sounds very simple—perhaps *too* simple, compared to our experience. How are we to listen for God's will, his "voice," if we have no prior experience of what he "sounds" like? How are we supposed to hear him when the pull and distractions of the world are so loud, so constant, and so compelling? How can we know that what we are hearing is really from him and not simply wish-fulfillment? How can we trust him if we find it difficult to trust people in general, or even to trust ourselves?

Theological hope has some things to say at this point that will keep us grounded and allow us to entrust ourselves to the necessary process of discernment. First of all, hope keeps us aware that God exists and that he in fact has a plan for us—that our lives are far from aimless but are tending toward a definite goal along a specific path that the Lord has mapped out for us. The Scriptures testify to this: "I know well the plans I have in mind for you," the Lord says through the prophet Jeremiah, "plans for your welfare and not for woe, so as to give you a future of hope" (Jer 29:11). Theological hope keeps us focused on the fact that, as we discern, it is not our responsibility to create our vocation or our life's path out of thin air, much less to search high and low for it as if God has hidden it out of our reach. On the contrary: God is waiting to reveal both himself and his plans to us, and hope points us in the right direction to receive this revelation.

Just as important, theological hope always tends toward eternal life as its ultimate object—that is, hope reminds us that we are destined, ultimately, for beatitude. This realization that God creates us and calls us to happiness gives us confidence that he is concerned for our good not only in the next life but in this life as well, and this allows us to trust the path God has marked out for us even when we cannot always see, from our own perspective, how a particular step may be good.

Blessed John Henry Newman, who became a Catholic in 1845 and a priest of the Oratory of Saint Philip Neri in 1848, was baptized in the Church of England and had been an Anglican clergyman for more than twenty years. To follow his conscience, and ultimately his vocation, as he discerned it over time, involved great personal sacrifice—he resigned his livelihood, left his home, was estranged from most of his friends and even much of his family, was publicly criticized in the press and from the pulpit, and for many months he was not even sure, having essentially left the Anglican Church, whether he could enter the Catholic Church or not. Several decades later, he composed a series of *Meditations on Christian Doctrine*; in the first one, on "Hope in God [the] Creator," we can see the important perspective that the virtue of hope gave him toward his own vocation and his ability to trust God:

> God has created all things for good; all things for
> their greatest good; everything for its own good.

. . . God has determined, unless I interfere with His plan, that I should reach that which will be my greatest happiness. He looks on me individually, He calls me by my name, He knows what I can do, what I can best be, what is my greatest happiness, and He means to give it me.

God knows what is my greatest happiness, but I do not. . . . Thus God leads us by strange ways; we know He wills our happiness, but we neither know what our happiness is, nor the way. We are blind; left to ourselves we should take the wrong way; we must leave it to Him.

Let us put ourselves into His hands, and not be startled though He leads us by a strange way. . . . Let us be sure He will lead us right, that He will bring us to that which is, not indeed what we think best, nor what is best for another, but what is best for us.[3]

Hope also allows us to understand what discernment *is not*. Discernment does not mean planning for every worst-case scenario that could possibly happen in the state in life we are considering for ourselves and determining ahead of time that we have everything that we need to meet every eventuality. This is just impossible; for one thing, most of the scenarios we might envision are mutually exclusive, and so they couldn't possibly *all* happen; it would be a waste of time to try to plan for all of them. But, more

---

[3]   John Henry Newman, *Meditations and Devotions of the Late Cardinal Newman,* "Hope in God—Creator" (London: Longmans, Green and Co., 1907), 299–300.

importantly, theological hope trains us to rely on *God* to bring us along the path that leads to our goal and not on our own strength. What is important is not that we know what will happen but that *he* knows, not that we have the strength to face every challenge but that we stay close to him—and he is omnipotent, after all.

Again, Newman sees the importance of this aspect of hope:

> God has created me to do Him some definite service; He has committed some work to me which He has not committed to another. . . . He has not created me for naught. . . . Therefore I will trust Him. Whatever, wherever I am, I can never be thrown away.
>
> If I am in sickness, my sickness may serve Him; in perplexity, my perplexity may serve Him; if I am in sorrow, my sorrow may serve Him. My sickness, or perplexity, or sorrow may be necessary causes of some great end, which is quite beyond us. He does nothing in vain; He may prolong my life, He may shorten it; He knows what He is about. He may take away my friends, He may throw me among strangers, He may make me feel desolate, make my spirits sink, hide the future from me—still He knows what He is about.[4]

(That is, he knows what he is doing.)

So practicing the virtue of hope relative to our discernment means striving repeatedly to trust that God knows

---

[4]   Ibid., 301–2.

what he's doing, even when what we should do isn't quite clear to us; to trust that God has a plan for our lives, even when it isn't yet evident to us; to trust that God will be able to sustain us through all of the ups and downs that our future may bring, even if all that we may be able to anticipate at any particular moment are challenges that seem too daunting for us. When we rely on God's strength and not on ourselves—when we put our theological hope into practice—we are able also to exercise the virtue of *magnanimity* that we spoke of previously—that virtue of "large-heartedness" that allows us to respond generously to the greatness of the calling we have received. Of *course* what God is asking us to do goes beyond our abilities— but hopeful hearts are buoyed up by this fact because they know that the inherent challenge is also an opportunity to cooperate with God. The only reason to despair is if we convince ourselves that we are supposed to fulfill our vocations alone.

We must remember one more important fact, which is tied very closely to the fundamental nature of hope as the virtue of people who are "on the way" to the goal. Discernment is essentially important in youth in order to choose and enter into a state in life, but it does not end once we have committed ourselves to doing God's will. Although the moment of consecration, ordination, or marriage comes once, it must be lived out day by day, and this requires both a persevering conversion and a continued openness to listening for and discerning God's voice amid the changing circumstances of daily life. Often enough, the strength of our commitment—and the depth of our hope and trust in God—is tested when we least expect it.

Perhaps the best example of this is found in the household where the Lord himself came to make his dwelling on earth. Surely *there* discernment of God's will could not have been any easier—"the angel Gabriel was sent from God to . . . Nazareth" to announce to Mary in person exactly what God had planned for her and for her divine Child (Lk 1:26). Although the process was not quite as simple for her husband Joseph (cf. Mt 1:18ff), he too was given reassurance of the divine plan and precise instructions to follow in carrying it out, which he did immediately. The next few months in Nazareth must have been a joy: the baby who was destined to save the world was destined to rest in a crib and a cradle built in his adoptive father's own workshop; his mother busied her hands preparing linens and baby clothes and everything her child would need upon his appearance in their dusty town of Galilee.

And then, when everything was ready for him, and they had had plenty of time to prepare home and hearts and minds, everything changed. First, an imperial decree to travel ninety miles south—at precisely the wrong time for an expectant mother—to a tiny overcrowded village, to wander among strangers and to give birth in a borrowed stable. As if that weren't enough, just when they were adapting to their new situation, a new emergency arose that meant a journey through the desert, in the dark, with a murderous king's soldiers on their heels—hundreds of miles to a foreign land, where the carpenter had no friends or family, no job prospects, no place to live, no way to care for his family, and no idea when they would be able to come home. By the time they finally made it back to Nazareth, surely the child was too big for the crib on which his father had expended so much labor; surely he had outgrown all of the baby clothes his mother had woven and which he had never worn.

The British Catholic author Caryll Houselander (a hero of hope in her own right, whom we will have a chance to consider later) writes about this episode in the life of the Holy Family and how it reveals the way that God works not just in their lives but in ours as well. It has to do, she says, with the fact that all disciples are given the responsibility, like Our Lady, to let Christ make himself present in our lives—in a sense, to carry him with us wherever we go. This means that he must be in charge, not just of the general, overarching plan of our life, but of every step along the way. This is why God could alter even the plan that Our Lady and Saint Joseph thought that they had figured out:

> It is difficult to imagine that a plan like this—so full of sweet order, and prudence and commonsense, so harmless—could not be pleasing to God.
>
> Yet God changes everything. He sends us to where He wants to be; among those whom He wishes to be among; to do that which He wishes to do in our lives.[5]

---

5   Caryll Houselander, *The Passion of the Infant Christ* (London: Sheed & Ward, 1949).

We've got to be careful to make sure that we read that second paragraph correctly. Caryll Houselander says that if God changes things, it is in order to send us *where he wants to be*—not simply where he wants *us* to be. That is, he chooses our course precisely because he is coming with us, because he is dwelling in us—the interactions, the relationships, even the confrontations of each day, while sometimes confusing or challenging to us if we are only looking at them on the surface, may have the deeper purpose of bringing him, dwelling in us, to exactly the person who needs to encounter him and who wouldn't have had contact with him in any other way.

In the next section, we're going to learn about a missionary through whom many people encountered the Lord. This priest traveled halfway around the world, carrying the Gospel message in his heart, along with zeal and enthusiasm for sharing the gift of faith that he had received from an early age with those who had never had a chance to hear it. But it was not as easy to do this as he expected it would be, and it took a great deal of soul-searching—and a healthy dose of hope—for him to discern the precise way in which the Lord was leading him to share the Faith, his gifts, and himself with the people God had sent him to serve.

Submission of Mind and Will—
Saint Joseph Freinademetz

As a seminarian and then as a priest, I have often been asked to tell what most people would refer to as my "vocation story." This is a common experience, and the simple, direct way that the question is usually put seems to imply that many people think that such a story, for priests and religious at least, is usually a straightforward thing. When we're talking about the lives of the saints—I'm not one of *those*, by the way, though I'm trying to be—this wanting to keep things simple gets even worse. Centuries' worth of books about saints give us stories of holy children who become holy teens who become holy adults and never seem to have any doubts or worries or questions about what God wants them to do. Fortunately for us, however—though perhaps not always for them, at least not at the time—not all those who serve the Lord found discerning their vocations quite so straightforward, and for some, the path God had chosen for them took them places they could not have anticipated, both externally and internally.

Joseph Freinademetz was born in Oies, a little hamlet near the town of Abrei in the Dolomite mountains of the South Tyrol region of southern Austria, on April 15, 1852. He was the fourth of ten children in his family, who scraped out a meager living on a little farm in their remote mountain village. Their daily life was centered around family prayer and devotion—including a twenty-minute walk for the whole family to daily Mass—and each week Joseph's father made a weekly pilgrimage to the mountain chapel of the Holy Cross, a mile and a quarter above sea level, to pray for his family and for his children's future.

Not surprisingly, Joseph developed a deep love for God and for the Church from an early age, and after four years of elementary school, the parish priest in Abrei advised Joseph's parents to send him to the diocesan city of

Brixen, now known as Bressanone, for a chance at a better education with a view of a future vocation to the priesthood. Joseph was an average student in the elementary school and high school in Brixen but showed an extraordinary talent for ancient and modern languages. In 1872, he entered the diocesan seminary; at the behest of the local bishop, his professors encouraged all of their students to give thought to the work of missionaries throughout the world. In 1875, Joseph was ordained a priest for the Diocese of Brixen and began his ministry in the parish of Saint Martin's in the Gader Valley not far from his native village.

A few years later, the diocesan newsletter ran a notice about a new German-speaking missionary order, the Society of the Divine Word, which had been recently founded by Father Arnold Janssen in Steyl, Holland. Father Joseph made up his mind almost immediately to ask his bishop for permission to join the new order; within a few months, it had been granted, and in August 1878, he was received as one of the first Divine Word missionaries. Less than seven months after arriving in Steyl, Father Joseph and another missionary, Father John Baptist Anzer, embarked on March 15, 1879, for the mission territories in China.

Their first stop was Hong Kong, where they arrived on April 20, and where Italian missionaries who had been established there for many years gave them a two-year introduction to the language and culture of the country. In 1881, Father Joseph and his fellow Divine Word missionaries traveled north to Shangdong Province, a region along the east-central coast of China then under the

German sphere of influence. He was twenty-nine years old at the time and would serve in Shangdong for the rest of his life—a total of twenty-seven years, until his death in 1908 at the age of fifty-six.

When Father Joseph first left Saint Martin's, his parish in the Tyrol, to be a missionary, his parishioners could not have been happier for him. Tyrol was a thoroughly Catholic region—the parish priest was greeted warmly in the streets and children ran up to kiss his hand—and the idea that one of their own was going off to spread the Gospel they held so dear brought honor upon the whole town. In his farewell sermon to his parish, Father Joseph expressed his understanding of his vocation in words that may seem rather jarring to us today: "When I think of those unfortunate lands and peoples where the darkest night of paganism reigns, where the true religion is unknown, of those people who are also our brothers and sisters, my heart beats passionately and tears well up in my eyes. . . . I know the surpassing misery of our brothers across the oceans who, with tears in their eyes, stretch out their hands toward us, imploring help."[6]

In other words, Father Joseph went to China with a rather one-sided view of his missionary vocation: he was destined, he believed, to put God and faith into the Chinese people.

Upon arriving in Hong Kong for his missionary novitiate, he met with almost immediate disillusionment. The

6   Sepp Hollweck, *Joseph Freinademetz: Serving the People of China*, trans. Jacqueline Mulberge (Rome: Society of the Divine Word, 2003).

little mission church was shabby and in disrepair, and certainly looked worse in his eyes compared to the magnificent pagoda up the road, where most of the local residents gathered for festivals. The Italian missionary who was supposed to be training the new arrivals took advantage of their presence to visit the mission outposts on the neighboring islands, and Father Joseph was left alone for long stretches of time. When it was his turn, some months later, to evangelize in these remote missions, he met with little success; people would come once to see the new missionary from Europe, but it was for the novelty, not for his message. Most did not return, and he was more often greeted with shouts of "foreign devil!" as he walked the streets—a far cry from the children of the Gader Valley who used to run to kiss his hands.

Father Joseph spent much of his first year in a state of confusion about his vocation and, in many ways, a state of depression. His initial zeal for the missions seemed to be waning as he became increasingly disillusioned by one failure to connect after another, and he placed the blame for his lack of success squarely on the Chinese people, whom he considered incapable of receiving the message he had traveled so far to bring to them. "China is well and truly the kingdom of the devil," he wrote. "You can hardly go ten steps without coming up against all kinds of hellish images and every manner of devilry! . . . The Chinese character has little that appeals to us Europeans. . . . The Creator did not endow the Chinese with the same qualities as the Europeans. . . . The Chinese are incapable of higher motives."[7]

There is really no hiding the nature of these words and the sentiment that they convey—no putting them in context to explain them away. They are exactly what they seem to be: angry, bitter words, full of racism and gross prejudice. Clearly Joseph Freinademetz was no automatic saint, and we can only imagine the state of mind and frustration of spirit that would have led him, once so full of zeal and professing such love for the missions, to utter these words.

Yet, the next time that we see Father Joseph, a great transformation has taken place. He has exchanged his Roman-style black cassock for the blue robe of the mandarin; his reddish-blond beard and hair are dyed black, and he wears now a silk cap with a *queue* affixed at the back. He had taken great pains to learn the language of the people and had even begun to compose catechetical texts for them; in return, they were coming to him in ever greater numbers and had even given him a special name in Chinese—*Fú Shénfù*, "Fortunate Priest." When, in August 1886, he took his final, perpetual vows as a member of the Society of the Divine Word, he regarded it also as his definitive commitment to the Chinese missions. He wrote in his diary that day: "With this, brother Joseph, the die is cast: pray, work, suffer, endure. Your whole life for your beloved Chinese, then when you come to the evening of your life and lie on your deathbed, you can sleep

---

[7]   Ibid., 13.

surrounded by your dear Chinese. Adieu! Farewell forever dear homeland beyond the sea!"[8]

Around the same time, he had written home to his sister, "I assure you honestly and sincerely that I love China and the Chinese. . . . I want to live and die with the Chinese."[9]

Clearly, a great change has taken place in Father Joseph's attitude—indeed, this is a great understatement, as the testimony of his contemporaries makes clear. Some of his coworkers felt that his newfound affection for the Chinese was excessive and even wondered if it were simply for show; others worried that it would lead to his being taken advantage of and cheated. One of his superiors even questioned whether he could hear the confessions of the new Chinese converts fairly since his default attitude was to be so lenient with them, always considering them to be so holy by nature.

How can we explain such a transformation? As I mentioned, Father Joseph was no automatic saint, and the change did not come all at once. Frustratingly, he was not a very public person, either, so unlike someone like Saint Augustine, we have no detailed account of his emotions, no dramatic relation of a crisis of conversion. Only a few lines from Father Joseph, written in retrospect, give us a key to what must have happened in long hours of soul-searching and conversation with God during those difficult days in Hong Kong. In a little work called *The Missionary's Joys,* he explains, "If ever there was a great work on earth . . . it is the religion of the Crucified and the

---

9   Ibid.

apostolate inseparably connected with it. . . . In this light everything takes on a new, quite unique hue; what is small and unimportant becomes singularly attractive, what is bitter gains a peculiar sweetness."[10]

Here we begin to see and understand what was happening to Father Joseph in those days, and what was beginning to transform him not only into an effective missionary but into the man who would eventually be known as *Saint Joseph Freinademetz*—he was finding and using the theological virtue of hope. We have seen many times that the point of this theological virtue is to orient us, gradually and consistently, toward our ultimate goal, our eternal beatitude, the happiness of heaven. In the process, theological hope places all of our earthly hopes in their proper contexts: it prioritizes our wishes and desires according to their relationship to heaven. What gets us closer to eternal life takes priority, and what becomes an obstacle to friendship with God has to go.

The comments about the unconverted Chinese—that were so hard to listen to because they were so full of bitterness and prejudice—were likewise full of hopelessness. Because he was so focused on what he had always considered the measures of success and failure—outward marks of respect, large crowds in beautiful churches, a welcome reception to a message that seemed so self-evident to him—he was increasingly disillusioned when the people he had come to evangelize rejected his message. In his pain and sadness, it was easier to blame them

---

[10]   Ibid., 14.

for hardness of heart than to consider whether his evaluation of the situation had been correct.

Through some quiet intervention of Divine Providence, theological hope was able to overcome these seeds of despair. Rather than abandon the mission, Father Joseph persevered, not only in the work of the apostolate, but in the "great work" of prayer to Christ crucified. We will never know the content of the conversations that passed between them, but we see the effects: once theological hope took hold of Father Joseph's heart, it effected a complete reordering of his priorities.

Specifically, he was able to see how the vocation that he had discerned many years before in Austria—the call to be a missionary that he was sure he had heard clearly—was the way God had chosen for him to achieve salvation. Theological hope, which fixes our eyes on the goal, put this vocation first and everything else after it; Father Joseph hadn't come to China to have his hands kissed by adoring congregants but to preach the Gospel with all of his energy and strength. If that was what God sent him to do, then the virtue of hope allowed him to trust that God would give him the ability to do it.

Hope also allowed him, as he said, to see the great importance of things he had previously considered very small—to notice that God was already acting in hidden ways that Father Joseph had not appreciated up to now. For Father Joseph, this meant something very specific. He writes, "The main work still remains: transformation of the inner person: to study the Chinese way of thought, Chinese customs and usages, Chinese character and disposition. All that cannot be achieved in a day, not even in one year, and also not without some painful surgery."[11]

Father Joseph needed to replace his old attitude—that he had traveled halfway around the world to "put God into" the poor, misguided Chinese—with the truth that he was coming to understand with God's help: that the people among whom he was living possessed an incredibly ancient culture and philosophy, with a character and way of life that, while different from his own, was something valuable and worth building on. He needed to recognize that, as children of God, the people he was evangelizing were not "blank slates" and work instead to build on their traditions to lead them to a fuller appreciation of the truth of the Gospel. When he came to understand this, he was able to introduce Jesus Christ to them as the fulfillment of their hopes, and his hearers responded to him enthusiastically. This process of replacing his old attitudes with new understanding was difficult, however; it was truly the "painful surgery" of which he wrote, and it took repeated acts of theological hope for him to be convinced that it was possible and that it would ultimately be beneficial for him and for his mission.

The virtue of hope also allowed Father Joseph to persevere in the very practical task of acquiring this knowledge of Chinese ways, which were still so new to him. Hope reminds us that we are always "on the way" to our goal, and this realization ought to bring great consolation: it means that we are works in progress and that we have opportunities to progress. If the entire success or failure

---

[11]   Hollweck, *Joseph Freinademetz*, 14.

of Father Joseph's mission depended on whether he had "gotten it" by the moment when he wrote those first bitter words, he was doomed. And that, in fact, is what the sin of despair means—a choice to say, "This is it. This is as far as I go; this is as far as I am willing to believe my path goes. I refuse to believe that anything changes after this for me." It is a rejection of the possibility that God can do any more and a rejection of the possibility of doing any more in cooperation with God.

Hope, on the other hand, keeps its focus on the *status viatoris*, the state of being "on the way," and remembers that as long as we are alive we must keep moving toward the goal. Our progress may be slow—indeed, it may be slower than we like, it may be painfully tedious, even embarrassingly small if we compare it to others around us who seem to be moving quickly—but along with theological hope, we find other virtues that allow us to stay on the road: courage, perseverance, and, above all, patience. Father Joseph knew that his work of coming to know the Chinese culture would take time, but he was hopeful about his eventual success, and this hope allowed him to proceed step-by-step without losing heart.

One more comment from Saint Joseph can provide valuable insight for us as we try to hold on to hope while we discern and live out our own vocations amid the various twists and turns that life may bring. We mustn't forget that he was very far from home and that, while he was beginning to appreciate his new surroundings and culture more and more, it was still quite strange to him. It would be foolish in the extreme to forget how this feels or to think that it did not affect him; in fact, the contrary was true, as his words reveal. But he learned from the experience: "The quiet solitude and general loneliness speak to the heart of the missionary in a unique manner, and since the more we are alone, the closer God is to us, the missionary does not know whether in such a situation he should cry because of inner hurt or shout for great joy, and so he does both."[12]

Remember what we have learned about the object of theological hope: through this virtue, we learn to focus our attention on two things: on the eternal life which is our goal and on the help of God who is the only One who can help us to attain it. Saint Joseph experienced firsthand that loneliness was going to be part of his day-to-day life in the missions, especially in the early days when most people were not interested in his message. This was jarring and disappointing, coming as he did from an area where he had been so well-respected. But first the virtue of hope allowed him to recognize loneliness—which he describes also as solitude—as part of his vocation, his particular path to heaven, and therefore something full of purpose and meaning. It is still painful—it still causes inner hurt, as he admits—but it need not cause despair anymore.

More importantly, hope directs his attention to God as the source of help and strength for fulfilling his vocation, and so Saint Joseph was able to see even his moments of loneliness—perhaps even especially his moments of loneliness—as opportunities for closeness with God. Hope transformed what could have been reasons for sadness and

---

[12]   Ibid., 14.

despair into reasons for great rejoicing because it enabled Saint Joseph to realize just how near God really was to him. He learned this lesson half a world away from home, and it expanded his heart to include a whole nation. Next, we'll meet an extraordinary young man who learned a similar lesson in his own backyard when his heart was broken over the woman he loved.

Faith Shows the Path—Blessed Pier Giorgio Frassati

One important thing to remember about hope—like the other theological virtues—is that it is *infused* by God directly into the soul, given as a gift along with the sanctifying grace received at Baptism. Although we need to develop this virtue over time, the gift is ours from our earliest days, and becoming an expert in hope is a matter of practice and openness to the work of the Holy Spirit and not merely a matter of years. The next "hero of hope" whom we will consider was able to acquire a capacity for trusting and responding to God's will that seems well beyond his years, and that transformed his entire life, short as it was measured by earthly expectations.

Pier Giorgio Frassati was born April 6, 1901 in Turin, Italy. His father, Alfredo, was the founder and publisher of *La Stampa*, then, as now, one of the most important daily newspapers in the country, and was very influential in Italian politics. Signore Frassati served several terms in the Italian parliament as a senator and was appointed ambassador to Germany in the early 1920s. His wife, Adelaide Ametis, had high hopes for their son and for his sister Luciana, who was born the following year, and took great pains to see that they spent time at the "right" schools and among the "right" people. Unfortunately, their own relationship was rocky, and although they loved their children dearly, home life was often marked by a certain tension.

His father's success and influence meant that Pier Giorgio had a fairly comfortable situation, as far as his material needs were concerned, although his father was frugal and did not give his children much pocket money. Pier Giorgio learned from an early age, however, the importance of generosity and attentiveness to the needs of others. One story from his childhood recalls how, when he was only four years old, he went by himself to answer a knock at the front door of the house. There was a poor woman holding her young son, who was crying—she had come in search of money and something to eat. Pier Giorgio noticed that her son had bare feet and immediately took off his own socks and shoes to give to the boy who had none. This would continue throughout his life: years later, he returned home in freezing weather—it was about 10 degrees outside—without his new overcoat. When he told his father he had given it to a homeless man on the street, Alfredo was annoyed. Pier Giorgio simply shrugged his shoulders; "But you see, papa, it was cold," he said.

In 1918, when he was seventeen years old, Pier Giorgio joined the Saint Vincent de Paul Society, which is dedicated to serving the poor and the sick. He spent a great deal of his spare time visiting these people in their homes, taking them meals, giving gifts of money—often enough, out of his own pocket—buying them prescriptions, and simply spending time with them. He was often late for meals with his family, who chalked up his behavior to thought-lessness or what they presumed was his flighty character. In reality, most of the time he had given his car or train fare to some needy person he had met at the station, and he had walked or run home instead. He kept these acts of charity secret and persevered in them throughout his life, although ultimately they contributed to it being cut short. Pier Giorgio died in 1925, at the age of twenty-four, after contracting polio fever—probably from one of the sick people he visited through the St. Vincent de Paul Society. His family was shocked to see the thousands of poor mourners who lined the streets as his funeral procession passed by.

In Pier Giorgio's day, as in our own, to hear the description I have just given of such a young man almost inevitably would lead to one thought in the minds of most Catholics: "He should probably be a priest." It's a natural thought, I suppose: when we see outward generosity and devotion like his of course we know it's connected with holiness, and it's easy to over-simplify things and think that to be a holy young man you have to have a priestly or religious vocation. We would especially think this, perhaps, when I add that Pier Giorgio was going to Mass every day and spending long hours in prayer before the Blessed Sacrament. Nevertheless, he felt God's call leading him to embrace holiness in the lay state, in a secular vocation. He gave himself to this vocation with his characteristic generosity of spirit, and in the process, he became an example for all young people who answer the universal call to holiness in the midst of the world.

When he completed secondary school in 1918, Pier Giorgio enrolled to study mechanical engineering at the Royal Polytechnic of Turin. He had become aware of the harsh conditions faced by workers in the Italian mines, and so he decided to study mining engineering so that he could, he hoped, serve Christ by coming to the assistance of this exploited group.[13] He also became politically active in both Catholic workers' groups and Catholic student and youth organizations. Following in his father's footsteps, he took a leading role in publishing a Catholic daily newspaper, *Il Momento*, which disseminated Church social teaching and commented on current events in light of it.

But Pier Giorgio's life wasn't all hard work at school and in political clubs—far from it. He was an attractive, popular young man who made friends easily and was fiercely loyal to them, and he found himself at the center of a circle that called themselves *Gli Tipi Loschi*—which loosely translates to "The Shady Characters." His job among this group of young friends was to arrange practical jokes—which he took to with gusto, from all accounts—and he also served as scout and planner for their many weekend trips to the mountains around Turin. Pier Giorgio was an avid hiker, skier, and mountain climber, and his personal motto became *Verso l'alto*, "To the heights."

It was in the context of these trips to the mountains, in the company of the Shady Characters, that Pier Giorgio came to understand another aspect, he thought, of his

---

[13]   Maria DiLorenzo, *Blessed Pier Giorgio Frassati: An Ordinary Christian,* trans. Robert Ventresca (Boston: Pauline Books and Media, 2004), 25.

vocation. For, toward the end of 1924 (when he was twenty-three), Pier Giorgio fell in love . . . *deeply*. He had long been friends with Laura Hidalgo, the daughter of a Spanish government official and a mathematics student at the Polytechnic. Now, his feelings for her had grown much deeper, and Pier Giorgio was starting to think seriously about a future with Laura as his wife.

Only he never mentioned it to Laura. By this time, both of her parents had died, and in addition to attending school, Laura was working to support herself and her little brother. She was not what many people would consider particularly pretty—although to Pier Giorgio she was the most beautiful young woman around. She took part in Catholic Action and Catholic youth groups but was somewhat awkward at purely social occasions. She was, in a word, not the kind of person that Signora Frassati, the wife of a publisher, a senator, and an ambassador, was looking for to marry to her eldest and only son.

Pier Giorgio was well aware of this, and had no desire to add more tension to his parents' already-rocky marriage. He consulted an old priest friend of his, Father Antonio Cojazzi, to try to discern with him what God's will could be for him in this situation. Surely, the friendship that he had developed with Laura, which was now blossoming into something more, at least for Pier Giorgio, had arisen in good and holy circumstances. Surely, this must mean that it came from God? But the fact that his parents would oppose the match, and that this would become a source of bad feelings that would affect not only Pier Giorgio's relationship with them but their relationship with one another,

presented a serious obstacle for him and made it difficult for him to see how God could want him to proceed.
"To destroy one family in order to create another would
be absurd and is not even worth thinking about," Father
Antonio recalls Pier Giorgio telling him that day. "I will
pay the price, but God's will be done."[14]

Father Antonio discussed the matter at some length, and
the priest explained that, at the age of twenty-four, Pier
Giorgio had a right to decide for himself, even against his
parents' wishes. But he would not defy them, and so they
ended with the sad realization that the only thing to do
was to give up on the idea of pursuing a relationship with
Laura at all. As a last attempt to see if he might be wrong
about his impressions, Pier Giorgio invited Laura, along
with two other girls, to the house for tea one afternoon and
watched his mother and sister's reactions to her closely.
They were clearly not impressed, and after confiding in
his sister that afternoon, he decided to give up on his plans
of ever having a future with Laura and to keep his feelings
for her to himself, never having given her so much as a
hint as to how he felt.

Pier Giorgio never told anyone about this situation
during his lifetime, in fact, other than his sister and one
close friend, Isidoro Bonini. From his letters to Isidoro
over the next couple of months, we can get a sense of how
deeply things were affecting him:

(From December 28:)

Dearest Friend,

---

[14]   Quoted in Di Lorenzo, *Blessed Pier Giorgio Frassati*, 91.

I am reading Italo Mario Angeloni's romance novel "I Loved That Way" where he describes in the first part his love for an Andalusian woman and believe me I am moved because it seems like my own love story.

I too loved that way, only that in the novel it is the woman who makes the sacrifice whereas in my case I will be sacrificed. But if that is how God wants it, His Holy Will be done. . . .[15]

(And two weeks later)

Dearest friend,

. . . . Every day that passes by convinces me all the more how ugly the world is. . . .

[My life] is going through perhaps the most acute period of a grave crisis and right at this moment my sister is going far away and so it's left to me to be cheerful at home and to suppress the somber mood caused by all the various setbacks that are piling up against me. . . . I'll always be cheerful on the outside to demonstrate to our companions who don't share our idea that to be Catholic means to be joyful young people; but on the inside when I'm alone I give vent to my sadness.[16]

---

[15]   Pier Giorgio Frassati to Isidoro Bonini, 28 December 1924. In *Pier Giorgio Frassati: Letters to His Friends and Family*, trans. Fr. Timothy Deeter, ed. Fr. Timothy Deeter and Christine Wohar (New York: St Paul's, 2009), 190.

[16]   Pier Giorgio Frassati to Isidoro Bonini, 15 January 1925. In *Frassati: Letters*, 196–97.

All of this may seem a bit of self-indulgent carrying on by a young person with the not-so-rare condition of a broken heart. Compared to some of the trials and crises that we have heard about so far, Pier Giorgio's disappointment may seem small and even routine . . . and we may be tempted to roll our eyes and say, under our breath at least, "Get over it!" But bear with me . . . after all, few of us, hopefully, may have our hope tested in extreme conditions like serious addictions or unexpected challenges in foreign lands, but all of us need to learn to be hopeful amid the trials, large and small, of day-to-day life. And the lessons that Blessed Pier Giorgio learned through this apparently little trial are important ones.

Take that second letter, for example . . . the one about how ugly the world is. Even as Pier Giorgio reflects on his situation, he begins to realize something that sounds very much like what we have been talking about already: "Every now and then I ask myself: shall I go on trying to follow the right path? Will I have the good fortune to persevere to the end? In this tremendous clash of doubts, the Faith given to me in Baptism suggests to me with a sure voice: 'By yourself you can do nothing, but if you have God as the center of your every action, then, yes, you will reach the goal.'"[17]

Pier Giorgio is still focusing on his problem, but already he is beginning to look toward the possibility of getting through it, of "reaching the goal." It's important to note that he's not talking about getting what he wants—that is, a relationship with Laura—but arriving at the true goal

---

[17]   Ibid.

of his whole life, the destination that God has set up for him. It's not clear at this point that he's sure what that goal is, exactly, but he's sure that God knows, and that seems to be enough, at least for the time being. He takes up the same theme in another letter to Isidoro two weeks later:

> The struggle is hard, but it is also necessary to overcome and to find again our little road to Damascus so that we can march along it toward that Goal which we all should attain. . . . Will I have the strength to succeed? Certainly the Faith is still the sole anchor of salvation to which we must grasp strongly; without it what would our whole life be? Nothing, or better it would be spent uselessly; because in the world there is only sorrow, and sorrow without Faith is unbearable, while sorrow nourished by the torch of the Faith becomes a beautiful thing because it fortifies the soul in its struggles.[18]

Here we begin to see the particular contribution that Pier Giorgio can make to our discussion of theological hope. He is learning to trust, in the midst of his personal sacrifice and suffering, that God will see him through, that things will turn out well. He is exercising the virtue of hope, in other words, and drawing strength from it to persevere. But he is not being hopeful because he particularly *feels* it at the time—he is writing these letters while the pain is still fresh, yet he is already talking about struggling well. Rather, his ability to hope comes not from

---

[18]   Pier Giorgio Frassati to Isidoro Bonini, 29 January 1925. In *Frassati: Letters*, 205–6.

what he *feels* but from what he *knows*—he is recognizing the extremely important intersection of the virtue of hope with the theological virtue of faith. He *believes* in Divine Providence, and so he can wait patiently for Providence to take its course. He *believes* in God's goodness, and so he can hope for good things from God, trust that all things will work out for good, even if the present moment does not seem particularly good from his own perspective.

Around this time, Pier Giorgio's sister Luciana, who had recently been married and moved away, wrote to him. She knew of his feelings for Laura, and inquired in her letter to him how he was feeling. His response gives an indication of what an impact this realization had on Pier Giorgio's ability to accept God's will and to trust in him:

Dearest,

... You ask me whether I am in good spirits. How could I not be so? As long as Faith gives me strength I will always be joyful; every Catholic cannot but be joyful: sadness ought to be banished from Catholic souls. Sorrow is not sadness, which is a worse illness than any other. This illness is nearly always caused by atheism. But the purpose for which we have been created shows us the path, even if strewn with many thorns, it is not a sad path. It is joyful even in the face of sorrow.[19]

Has Pier Giorgio simply gone from weeping over his

---

[19]   Pier Giorgio Frassati to Luciana Frassati Gawronski, 14 February 1925. In *Frassati: Letters*, 210.

sorrows to papering over them as if they're no longer important? Quite the contrary. His firm belief that God has a plan now enables him to try to see even his sufferings as part of that plan—as "thorns" along his "path." And the place that he identifies for his sufferings in God's plan is extraordinarily insightful for a young man his age:

> In today's struggles, I cannot but thank God because He has willed in His infinite Mercy to grant this sorrow to my heart so that by means of these arduous thorns I might return to a life that is more interior, more spiritual. Until this age, I was living too materially and now I need to refortify my soul for future struggles because from now on every day, every hour there will be a new battle to fight and a new victory to conquer. A spiritual upheaval must take place in me.[20]

So, the various struggles that life may bring to us have this in common, according to Pier Giorgio: they lead, if we face them well, to purity of heart and an ever deeper trust in God. This becomes possible if we start with faith in God's goodness, which informs and undergirds our ability to trust and hope in him. Of course, this leads naturally to an intersection with the third theological virtue, as Blessed Pier Giorgio is also quick to point out in his letters:

---

[20]   Pier Giorgio Frassati to Isidoro Bonini, 29 January 1925. In *Frassati: Letters*, 205–06.

As Catholics, we have a Love which surpasses every other love and which after that owed to God is immensely beautiful, just as our religion is beautiful. . . . It is indeed that which can be a guide and direction for our whole life, for a whole program. This, with the grace of God, can be the goal toward which my soul can strive. And so at first we are dismayed, because it is a beautiful plan, but a hard one, full of thorns and not many roses, but we trust in Divine Providence and in His Mercy.[21]

This was a moment of intense prayer and reflection for Pier Giorgio about the direction of his life; that is, about his vocation. He emerged from this incident with an expanded magnanimity—a new willingness to be great-hearted and generous, from which all of his friends benefited, including Laura, Isidoro, and the many poor and sick people whom he continued to visit without drawing attention to himself. He was also determined to be more receptive to God's will, to respond more immediately and unquestioningly, to try to focus on the Lord's desires and plans rather than his own. He was ready to be led by the Lord, wherever his future path would take him—as we know, that path turned out to be much shorter than anyone on earth could have anticipated, as Pier Giorgio succumbed to poliomyelitis in early July.

Who can say, really, what constitutes a great trial or a small one except the person who is going through it? We

---

[21] Pier Giorgio Frassati to Isidoro Bonini, 6 March 1925. In *Frassati: Letters*, 215–16.

mustn't underestimate the impact that this episode had in the life of Blessed Pier Giorgio simply because it seems routine to us—if nothing else, his prayer and reflection during this time, and the insights he gained from them, bore great fruit for himself and for us. In the next chapter, we will consider the stories of several men and women whose hope was tested in rather more difficult circumstances and who relied on God's grace and strength to endure both mental and physical suffering. Once again we will have reasons to be grateful for the communion of saints, in which we may all benefit from the wisdom gained firsthand by these heroes of hope, who relied on the Lord in moments of crisis and share their lessons with us.

4

We Dare to Struggle

Walking the Way of the Cross—Saint Josephine Bakhita

In the last chapter, we were talking about Blessed Pier
Giorgio's insight that the way that the Lord has marked
out for us may be a path bordered with thorns—that is,
it may involve pain and suffering. For Pier Giorgio, at
least, this was the key to making sense of life in a broken
world—the idea that the struggles that are part of daily life
are not something random or arbitrary but are, in fact, part
of the plan, and that within that plan they acquire meaning
and purpose. A hopeful outlook that allows us to integrate
these trials without losing trust in God keeps us off the
rocks of despair and enables us to accept even sorrowful
moments without becoming despondent.

Yet we know from experience that there are some people who simply cannot accept this explanation under any
circumstances—and that there are large numbers of other
people (perhaps including ourselves) who question it at
least from time to time. They reject it not because they

are not strong enough to bear up under the suffering but for quite the opposite reason: because they rail against it with all of their might, because they are fiercely opposed to the idea that suffering and pain would be part of any plan proposed by a God who claims to be benevolent and omnipotent. Because, in a word, it does not seem *just*.

The question of why evil should be present in a world where God is omnipotent and good—why the innocent should suffer while the wicked prosper, why those who serve the Lord should weep with their prayers unanswered—has affected and afflicted humanity for countless generations. The impact of such questions on the people of our modern era—who all too often try to find answers without really knowing where to look for them—is present all around us. Pope Benedict explains in his encyclical on hope:

> The atheism of the nineteenth and twentieth centuries is . . . a protest against the injustices of the world and of world history. A world marked by so much injustice, innocent suffering, and cynicism of power cannot be the work of a good God. A God with responsibility for such a world would not be a just God, much less a good God. It is for the sake of morality that this God has to be contested.
>
> Since there is no God to create justice, it seems man himself is now called to establish justice. . . . It is no accident that this idea has led to the greatest forms of cruelty and violations of justice. . . . A

world which has to create its own justice is a world
without hope.[1]

In the Holy Father's description, we see very a dramatic
portrayal of an attitude that we may become susceptible
to in more subtle ways day by day. Like the person who
points to the injustices he perceives in the world as reasons to claim that God is absent or, worse, that God is a
fraud, it is tempting at times to isolate this or that trial or
challenge, this particular thorn on the path, and convince
ourselves that, in this case at least, God simply does not
care or does not understand.

The problem with this attitude is not that one cannot
sympathize with the feeling under the circumstances but
rather the direction in which such thinking invariably
leads. The next step in such a train of thought is to console
oneself for being hard done by and misunderstood; then
to question why such a thing should have happened to
begin with. The process leads, ineluctably, to resentment
for having had to face the trial in the first place, resentment of the scoundrel who plotted the path through the
thorn bushes that tore at such a one as I. It leads, in other
words, to the other great sin against hope: not despair, but
presumption.

What is the answer to such a dangerous and subtle
temptation? After all, the initial impulse is correct—there
are grave injustices in the world, which are clearly *not* in
accord with the will of the omnipotent Creator of all. How
is it possible to maintain faith in God and his justice in the

---

[1]   Benedict XVI, *Spe Salvi*, 42.

midst of such brokenness without becoming despondent nor proud?

In the late eleventh century, Bruno of Cologne, an influential churchman in the Diocese of Reims in northeastern France, gathered a group of six friends and founded a hermitage in the mountainous region named Chartreuse, not far from Grenoble. There they lived in silence and poverty, interceding for the world they had left behind and carrying out works of prayer and penance. Their desire to separate themselves from this broken world is as relevant today as it was then, as does the motto that the new Carthusians, as they came to be called, adopted for themselves: *Stat crux dum volvitur orbis*, "The Cross stands still while the world turns." Pope Benedict explains how only the Cross, and Christ crucified, allows us to stay hopeful amid the swirling injustices of the revolving world:

> In him who was crucified . . . God now reveals his true face in the figure of the sufferer who shares man's God-forsaken condition by taking it upon himself. This innocent sufferer has attained the certitude of hope: there is a God, and God can create justice in a way that we cannot conceive. . . .
>
> To protest against God in the name of justice is not helpful. A world without God is a world without hope (cf. Eph 2:12). Only God can create justice. And faith gives us the certainty that he does so. . . . God is justice and creates justice. This is our consolation and our hope.[2]

---

2   Ibid., 43, 44.

The justice that the Lord offers to us is a mysterious one, to be sure. He does not obliterate what he has created—for he created all things good, and although free creatures have strayed from his plan, his love for them, *for us*, is constant. He does not wipe things out and start over . . . and this is a sign not of his weakness but of the strength of his love. He creates justice in this world of sin in a way that is totally unheard of: by entering into it, taking all of the injustices of sinful men on his own shoulders, and *loving us to the end.* In the process, he gives us a new reason to hope: Yes, the path of our lives, since it passes through this world, is a path strewn with thorns. Yes, the path of our lives is a Way of Sorrows. But because our path is the Way of the Cross, at no time are we expected to walk it alone. He who calls us *to* the Cross, calls us *from* the Cross, and the saints, the real heroes of hope, are those who have the courage to walk the Way of the Cross in union with him.

Among the heroes of hope that Pope Benedict singles out in his encyclical *Spe Salvi* is a nineteenth-century girl from the Darfur region of Sudan. Born around 1869, at the age of nine, she was captured by Muslim slave traders while playing in the fields not far from her home in the village of Olgossa near Mount Agilerei. She was so terrified by her situation that she could not speak and even forgot her own name; her kidnappers began to call her Bakhita, which means "lucky one" in Arabic.

Bakhita and another girl managed to escape from her first captors. They were soon found walking by themselves, however, and taken captive by a different slaver, who forced Bakhita to walk about six hundred miles to El Obeid, an important trading city in the center of the country; she was sold twice more before she arrived there. In El Obeid, Bakhita was bought by a rich Arab merchant and became a maid in the family home.

In general, the merchant and his family treated Bakhita relatively well. However, after some accident—perhaps a broken vase or something similar—one of the merchant's sons beat and kicked her so severely that she was unable to get out of bed for over a month. Not long after this incident, Bakhita was sold again, this time to a general in the Turkish forces. She had to serve his wife and her mother, who both treated all the slaves very cruelly. In her autobiography, Bakhita recalls that hardly a day went by in that house that did not involve a beating or an injury of some kind. "When a wound from the whip began to heal," she wrote, "other blows would pour down on me, even though I had done nothing to deserve them."[3] Worst of all, she and her fellow slaves were marked by a process of tattooing and scarification, as 114 intricate patterns were cut with razors into her breasts, abdomen, and right arm, and the wounds filled with salt to create permanent scars.

In 1882, when a revolution threatened El Obeid, the general sold all but ten of his slaves and moved the household to the capital, Khartoum. It was there, in 1883, that Bakhita was sold to Callisto Legnani, the vice consul of the Italian government, who was by all accounts a very kind man. When Legnani left Sudan two years later,

---

[3] Maria Luisa Dagnino, *Bakhita Tells Her Story,* Third edition (Rome: Canossian Daughters of Charity, 1993), 49.

Bakhita, now about fifteen, begged to go with him. They arrived in Genoa in April 1885, and Legnani gave Bakhita to his friends Augusto and Maria Michieli, who had escaped from Khartoum with him. The Michieli family lived in a villa not far from the city of Venice, and Bakhita became a maid in their home and a nanny for their daughter Alice, known as Mimmina, who was born the following February.

Bakhita remained with the family in Venice for three years. Meanwhile, the revolutionary situation in Sudan had become less volatile, and Signore Michieli was able to return to see to the management of a hotel property he had acquired there before he had been forced to evacuate. He decided to sell the family estate in Venice and relocate permanently to Sudan, but arrangements were taking longer than expected, and at a certain point in 1888, Signora Michieli needed to travel to Sudan to assist her husband with some of the details. In late November, she left Bakhita and Mimmina in the care of the Canossian Daughters of Charity, a convent of Sisters in Venice whose order had been founded about fifty years earlier.

After about ten months, Signora Michieli returned to Venice and appeared at the convent to collect Bakhita and Mimmina, intending to take them to Sudan. But something had happened in the meantime that she could never have anticipated. While Signora Michieli was away, Bakhita came to understand who God was—and she experienced this as an encounter with Someone whom she had known since her childhood, without knowing who he was. As she recounts in her biography, "I remembered how, as a child, when I contemplated the sun, the moon, the stars, and all the beautiful things of nature, I was wondering, 'who is the master of it all?' And I felt a keen desire to see Him, know Him and pay Him homage. Now, at last, I knew Him."[4] Of her own accord, Bakhita had asked to be instructed in the Catholic faith and had enrolled in the Institute for Catechumens conducted by the Sisters in order to prepare for the reception of Baptism.

So, when Signora Michieli came to take her from the convent, Bakhita politely but firmly refused. "I love the Signora dearly, and to part from Mimmina cuts me to the heart. But I shall not leave this place because I cannot risk losing God."[5] Signora Michieli argued her case for three days, and eventually both the patriarch of Venice and the civil authorities were consulted. They arrived at the conclusion that since slavery had been outlawed in Italy almost a century earlier, Bakhita had never "belonged" to the Michielis and that since she was of legal age to determine her own affairs, it was up to Bakhita to decide whether to be baptized and whether or not to leave the convent.

Bakhita completed her preparation as a catechumen and was baptized on January 9, 1890 with the Christian names Giuseppina Margherita (Josephine Margaret). She continued to live in the convent with the Sisters, and soon made that situation permanent: in 1893, she began her novitiate in the community, and on December 8, 1896, she professed

---

4   Ibid., 61.

5   Anne Ball, *Modern Saints: Their Lives and Faces*, Book Two (Rockford, IL: TAN Books, 1990), 441.

her vows as a Canossian Daughter of Charity. In 1902, she was assigned to their convent at Schio in the province of Vicenza in northern Italy, where she spent the remaining forty-two years of her life. She became well-known for her kindness and gentle presence, and the inhabitants of Schio still refer to her as their *Madre Moretta,* their "Black Mother." After her life story was first published in 1931, Sister Josephine visited various communities throughout Italy, encouraging the Sisters, raising awareness of their mission, and asking for donations to support the work of the order. Calls for her canonization followed almost immediately upon her death on February 8, 1947, and the official process began just twelve years later.

Pope Benedict writes of the tremendous impact that those few months in the convent in Venice had upon this remarkable young woman, who had struggled so much in her life and faced so many seemingly hopeless situations:

> Here, after the terrifying "masters" who had owned her up to that point, Bakhita came to know a totally different kind of "master"—in Venetian dialect, which she was now learning, she used the name *"paron"* for the living God, the God of Jesus Christ.
>
> Up to that time she had known only masters who despised and maltreated her, or at best considered her a useful slave. Now, however, she heard that there is a *"paron"* above all masters, the Lord of all lords, and that this Lord is good, goodness in person. She came to know that this Lord even knew her, that he had created her—that he actually loved her. She

too was loved, and by none other than the supreme
"*Paron*", before whom all other masters are themselves no more than lowly servants. She was known
and loved and she was awaited.[6]

Here again we see the power of theological hope to
reveal the truth of the divine plan and, in the process, to
reorient one's whole outlook toward earthly things. The
gift that Bakhita was given through her encounter with
God—the encounter that led to the fullness of faith and
the fulfillment of her hopes—was real, lasting freedom.
She was not merely set free from earthly masters; she was
now free from fear, from sadness, from terrifying memo-
ries, from an uncertain future—all because she was at last
sure of who God was and where to find him.

The reality of this freedom had to be very "good news"
indeed to someone who had been literally enslaved for
so long. Yet, as soon as she experiences this freedom,
of her own accord, she expresses her newfound joy and
hope in terms of servitude and submission. She exchanges
one master for another: she calls God her divine *Paron*.
How can this be right? Certainly there are many names
she could have happily used for God—"Father," "Shepherd," "Beloved," even "Lord." But to call him "Master"
so quickly perhaps seems too much.

This is because we are thinking from a wounded human
perspective rather than trying to see with the eyes that
theological hope provides. Through her encounter with
God—and especially with the Son of God who has come

---

[6]   Benedict XVI, *Spe Salvi*, 3.

into the world to reveal the love of the Father for suffering humanity—Bakhita was able to see the path along which she, and all of the human race, are meant to travel toward eternal life. She was able to recognize the path of hope, in other words, and that was not all . . . she was able to see that it is likewise the Way of the Cross and that, even as every disciple is commanded to walk it, no one is expected to walk it alone. Pope Benedict continues his explanation of what Bakhita saw: "What is more, this master had himself accepted the destiny of being flogged and now he was waiting for her 'at the Father's right hand'. Now she had 'hope' —no longer simply the modest hope of finding masters who would be less cruel, but the great hope: 'I am definitively loved and whatever happens to me—I am awaited by this Love. And so my life is good.'"[7]

Bakhita was unfraid, and unashamed, to submit herself freely to her divine *Paron,* because in Christ she saw the Master who had himself become "the slave of all" (Mk 10:44). She was willing to become like him who had first become like her; she recognized her own wounds in his scourging at the pillar, her own insults and beatings in the torments that he endured during his passion. Theological hope allowed her to trust that the Lord who had endured so much for her sake, and had brought her so far already, would continue to give her strength to face whatever might come. She did not know what her future would bring, but she knew now that as long as she was "on the way," she needed to be walking that way in company with Christ.

This is the great message of hope that comes to us from

---

[7]   Ibid.

the Christian faith in the Incarnation of the Word of God: that we never walk the way alone, not even the way of suffering. The Incarnation—the truth that God has come in the flesh, that the eternal Son of God has appeared on earth, that he has a true human nature which is perfectly united to his true divine nature—reassures us that Jesus Christ knows exactly who we are, how we feel, what we need, and even how we suffer. It is too tempting sometimes to discount the sufferings that Christ endured—whether the day-to-day realities of fatigue, hunger, and thirst; the emotional strain of rejection and misunderstanding; the spiritual battles with temptation and the forces of evil; or the extreme pain and torture of his passion and death—by assuming that because he is a Divine Person, he is some-how immune to "real" suffering, that somehow it all came easy to him.

Faith tells us differently, though. Jesus Christ has a real human body, with all the working parts. He has a real human soul, with a real intellect and a real will that are free and sharp and perceptive—and that therefore feel things deeply. He has a real human heart, with real human emotions. He has a real human family, and real human friends, and loves them more deeply and more sincerely than anyone else we have ever known. The letter to the Hebrews says that he can "sympathize with our weak-nesses" because he "has similarly been tested in every way, yet without sin" (Heb 4:15). In a word, he truly knows what it is like to be us.

This is, or it ought to be, a great consolation in those moments when we feel like we are struggling alone and that we are misunderstood. In the face of any temptation, of any challenge or any pain, we may have absolute confidence that Christ understands exactly what we are going through and that he is able to give us precisely the assistance that we need in that moment. Moreover, he knows what we need, not from the perspective of some great cosmic observer looking down from on high yet unaffected by the turmoil of the world, but as one who walks the path beside us and knows the way by experience.

Still, we know that there are many things that stand in the way of our responding as we should to his call, and his will. Some of them come from our own "incarnation," so to speak, the fact that we ourselves are a composite of body and soul. In the next section, we might as well start with the most uncomfortable of them—fear— and get it out of the way. To do so, we'll learn from a woman who spent a lot of time being very afraid of some pretty scary things and found out that that wasn't such a bad idea after all.

The Courage to Be Afraid—Caryll Houselander

The next "hero of hope" we're going to consider liked to laugh . . . which is a good thing, because if she were able to overhear us making the suggestion that she was in any way heroic, she would have found it quite funny indeed. Never in the best of health, always a little bit nervous and awkward, she nevertheless became a source of strength and comfort for people weighed down by all sorts of anxiety and pain—as one eminent psychologist, a friend of hers, once put it, "She loved them back to life."[8] Like Saint Paul, she was able to find strength once she was able to admit her own weakness and figured out how to be brave enough to be afraid.

Frances Caryll Houselander was born in Bath, England on October 29, 1901, the second of two daughters in a rather troubled home. Born at home, she was terribly sick and weak that first day, so much so that her mother and uncle thought that she would not survive and called the local Anglican priest to come to the house for her christening. This early ill health foreshadowed many weaknesses and afflictions, both physical and emotional, that Caryll would face throughout her life. Although she attended several boarding schools, her frequent illnesses meant that her formal education was spotty at best.

The Houselanders' marriage had never been a particularly happy one, and Caryll's parents divorced when she was nine years old. Her father, Wilmot, was an atheist; her mother, Gertrude, in contrast, became increasingly pious and encouraged numerous outward devotions in her daughters as well. When Caryll was six years old, her mother was received into the Catholic Church, and her daughters with her; for this reason, Caryll sometimes referred to herself as a "rocking horse Catholic" rather than a "cradle Catholic" (that is, a Catholic from birth). Her later writings reveal that her relationship with God and her understanding of the sacraments was developing rapidly during her childhood; unfortunately, a series of

---

8   Eric Strauss, quoted in Maisie Ward, *Caryll Houselander, That Divine Eccentric* (New York: Sheed and Ward, 1962), 263.

incidents in her late teenage years led to her becoming estranged from the Catholic Church for about eight years. During this time, she investigated other Churches, searching for some way to keep her connection with God alive. She also began a love affair with the famous British spy Sidney Reilly, who some have suggested was Ian Fleming's inspiration for James Bond. The affair continued for several years, until Reilly broke it off and married another woman; Caryll herself would never marry.

What also happened to Caryll during this time of her being "out of the church"—and what may have helped to lead her back into it—was a succession of deep mystical experiences. She describes two of them in her writings. In one, she saw a vision of the crowned and crucified Christ in the sky over her neighborhood. His face, she realized the next day, was that of the Russian czar, who had been assassinated at the time that the vision had taken place. In another, while riding the train she suddenly perceived the face of Christ in the faces of all of the people surrounding her—not only on the train, but on the streets as well, all the way home and for a day or two after. These visions, and similar experiences in prayer, convinced her of the truth that every human being shares in the life of Christ—that, in fact, Jesus is living his life in the lives of men and women around the world. She began to live each day, and each relationship, as an encounter with Christ in others and as a sharing in what she referred to as "the Christ-life."

Although, as I have noted, Caryll's formal education was sporadic, but she had always shown a great skill for art, particularly with wood carving. Having moved out on her own, she began to earn her living carving religious artwork, particularly Nativity scenes, and making woodblocks for printing. She had also developed a talent for writing, and she often volunteered to contribute to the newsletters and magazines published by the various Catholic charitable organizations in which she took part. Although she did not consider herself a role model or a particularly holy person, Caryll's friends encouraged her to become an author in her own right and to share her theological insights with others in a more developed form. Her first book, *This War is the Passion*, was a collection of some of her articles on suffering with Christ and was published in 1941, two years into Britain's involvement in World War II. More than a dozen books would follow— including volumes of poetry, children's stories, and even a novel—before her early death from cancer in 1954.

Caryll lived in London during World War II, and like all the inhabitants of that city, suffered both physically and emotionally from the ravages of the Blitz. Between September 7, 1940 and May 10, 1941, the German Luftwaffe bombed London almost every night; more than a million London houses were destroyed or damaged, and more than twenty thousand civilians were killed in the city. As we have noted, from the time she was a girl, Caryll had always suffered from a weak physical condition and terrible nerves; for her even more than for most, the strain of the bombing was nearly unbearable. It was made even worse by the fact that she had duties at first aid stations and other civil defense assignments that meant she was often caught outside of air raid shelters when the attacks began.

A few years after the War, Caryll wrote to a friend of hers who was struggling with anxiety and confided in her the secret she had learned to surviving the Blitz:

> During the war I was simply terrified by air raids, and it was my lot to be in every one that happened in London—sometimes on the roofs of these flats, sometimes in the hospital. . . . I tried to build up my courage by reason and prayer, etc. Then one day I realized quite suddenly: As long as I try not to be afraid I shall be worse, and I shall show it one day and break; what God is asking of me, to do for suffering humanity, is to be afraid, to accept it and put up with it, as one has to put up with pain . . . or anything else.[9]

Perhaps you can remember, from a previous chapter, the curious little definition that Saint Thomas Aquinas gave of the object of hope: "the object of hope conceived broadly is a future good that is demanding but possible."[10] It seems that Caryll Houselander's secret to finding hope while the bombs were falling was to remember that hope

[9]   Caryll Houselander to Lois Boardman, 7 August 1949. In *The Letters of Caryll Houselander: Her Spiritual Legacy*, ed. Maisie Ward (New York: Sheed and Ward, 1965), 177–78.

[10]   Thomas Aquinas, *Quaestio disputata de spe*, iv. In *Disputed Questions on Virtue* [The Hackett Aquinas], trans. Jeffrey Hause and Clausia Eisen Murphy (Indianapolis: Hackett, 2010), 220.

allows us to keep going in situations that are arduous and difficult. This insight—startling to some, refreshing and freeing to others—that the object of our hope is something that is *supposed to be* demanding, is *supposed to be* fearful or tough or difficult to obtain, applies to our daily trials as well and is an important one to keep in mind. It is when we resent the fact that things are rough, or demand that they ought not to be, or try to get out of it, that we get into trouble. When we accept as a starting point that such and such a trial is going to be just that—a trial—then we can face it head-on with the strength that comes from hoping in God.

Pope Benedict makes a similar point in his encyclical on hope, where he calls suffering a setting for learning hope. Suffering, he explains, is an unavoidable part of human life because it comes from the fact that human beings are finite; that is, limited, and not in control of external circumstances. Moreover, sufferings arise from the sins of human beings which have built up over the course of history and led to the unjust situations that exist in our own day. While we can, and must, reduce suffering to a certain extent, we can never eliminate it completely, as long as we are living in this finite, broken world.

Hope, which we have seen many times is our necessary virtue while we are "on the way" through this world, allows us to persevere in the midst of sufferings and to trust in God's love and God's justice without losing heart. In a paradoxical way, the Holy Father suggests, to try to escape the brokenness of the world is to walk away from

God, who enters human history to take "away the sin of the world" (Jn 1:29) and to bring healing:

> It is when we attempt to avoid suffering by with-drawing from anything that might involve hurt, when we try to spare ourselves the effort and pain of pursuing truth, love, and goodness, that we drift into a life of emptiness, in which there may be almost no pain, but the dark sensation of meaninglessness and abandonment is all the greater. It is not by sidestep-ping or fleeing from suffering that we are healed, but rather by our capacity for accepting it, maturing through it and finding meaning through union with Christ, who suffered with infinite love.[11]

Caryll Houselander learned, from difficult experience, that to try to avoid her fear—which was, after all, a per-fectly appropriate reaction to the fact that high-explosive bombs were bursting all around her!—was simply leav-ing her exhausted, tense, and feeling very much alone. Although on one level she probably did not *feel* like she had any courage at all, when she was able to be brave enough to be afraid, everything fell into place. Because she was not avoiding the fear—her specific suffering in that moment—she also was not avoiding Christ, who desired to show her *compassion*: to suffer that fear with her. "From that hour [she writes] it became easy. I *was* terrified, but I was also perfectly conscious of being held in God's hands; before, I was too tensed up to feel them.

---

[11]   Benedict XVI, *Spe Salvi*, 37.

From the moment I just let go, I *knew* I was held up, and there was nothing more to worry about."[12]

> Instead of kidding myself and trying to minimize the danger or to find some distraction from it, I said to myself: "For as long as this raid lasts—an hour—or eight hours—you are going to be terrified . . . so you must just carry on and *be* terrified, that's all"—and at once the *strain* ceased. Oh yes, I was terrified; I've often had to resort to sheer force to hide the fact that my teeth were chattering. . . . But at the same time I felt that God had put his hand right down through all the well upon well of darkness and horror between Him and me and was holding the central point of my soul; and I knew that *however* afraid I was then, it would not, even could not, break me.[13]

What's really marvelous is the impact that this change in outlook had on Caryll's whole personality and demeanor. It allowed her not only to face the things that frightened her but also to take on more responsibilities, knowing that in doing so, she was cooperating with Christ: "I always volunteered (after this discovery) for *most* frightful things (if called on to do so only!)—like Mobile First Aid in the street, and fire watching on the roof of Nell Gwynn: and always knew God was there in a special way, to accept the

---

[12]   Caryll Houselander to Lois Boardman, 7 August 1949. In *Letters*, 177–78.

[13]   Caryll Houselander to Lois Boardman, 9 November 1949. In *Letters*, 183–84.

offering of fear. It's only when we try *not* to experience our special suffering that it can really break us."[14]

Of course, this insight is as old as the Scriptures, although then as now not everyone has eyes to see it. Weeks—and miles—before Jesus and his apostles ever arrived in Jerusalem for Holy Week, he spoke to them of his impending passion and death. "The Son of Man must suffer greatly and be rejected," he told them, "and be killed and on the third day be raised" (Lk 9:22). Immediately after this, "he said to all, 'If anyone wishes to come after me, he must deny himself and take up his cross daily and follow me" (9:23). Two realities are present in the Lord's words to his disciples: First, he was giving everyone who was following him plenty of warning, plenty of opportunity to consider if this was what they had signed up for; to decide whether they wanted to go with him any farther. If they were coming to Jerusalem with him, they would see him suffer and would most likely be called upon to suffer with him. But, more importantly, his predictions, so far in advance, indicated that he knew well the path that lay ahead—that it would not catch him by surprise. He was ready for it, and would be with his disciples as they bore their own crosses.

However, time and again, when the Lord mentions his passion, even to the Apostles, more often than not they change the subject or act as if they did not hear what he said to them. They are unable to benefit from his words to them, because they are unwilling to face their own fears. In this, as in so many situations in the Gospels, the Apostles

---

[14]   Ibid.

show us our own attitudes and behaviors in sharp relief. Caryll Houselander is familiar with this kind of response to the challenge of daily crosses and suggests the way in which we ought to overcome it: "In circumstances, so common in our times, in which we are faced with blatant physical danger, we tend to be concerned with how to save face, to make a good impression on ourselves and on others, to *hide* our fear at all costs, if possible even to appear heroic!"[15]

We recognize the truth in these words in the story that Saint Matthew records (Mt 20:17–28), when Jesus, on the way up to Jerusalem for Passover, once again mentions his passion to the twelve Apostles. On this occasion, not only do they not speak to him about what will happen; instead, they get into an argument among themselves over which one of them is the greatest. They try to cover up their fear by finding ways to be appear strongest and most important. Caryll Houselander continues:

> The attitude "I am not afraid," or, "I can overcome fear alone, by my own will," is wrong; and it is wrong because it is vanity. The attitude of humility is: "Yes, I am afraid, and while this thing lasts I shall be afraid and I shall suffer, but it is perfectly just that I should, and in any case, I am in the hands of God, Who knows me just as I am, with all my sins and follies, but nevertheless loves me infinitely."

15   Caryll Houselander, *The Comforting of Christ* (New York: Sheed and Ward, 1947), 149–50.

The stress passes immediately from self to God,
the tension is relaxed in the thought of God, and we
are carried through in His arms.[16]

The possibility of acting with such an attitude of humility is intimately connected with the virtue of hope, which, as we have noted several times already, allows us to see things as they really are: to keep our eyes fixed on heaven and to see the things of earth in proper perspective. Of course, this means seeing *ourselves*, as creatures of earth, in proper perspective as well, in relationship to God the Creator. Humility does not mean that we look on ourselves as worthless or consider ourselves the worst sinners in the world—indeed, this is the worst kind of false humility: really just pride dressed up in dirty clothes, which draws attention to itself for low reasons instead of lofty ones. Rather, true humility acknowledges the truth of how things stand: as finite creatures, we are totally dependent on God for help, and as creatures made in the image and likeness of a loving God, and called by him to friendship, we confidently hope that he will provide that help to us. When we are able to see the truth, and trust with hope, we draw new strength from our relationship with our loving Creator.

In an address on hope, one of only three General Audience talks he was able to give during his month-long tenure as bishop of Rome, Pope John Paul I expressed the reasons for our humble confidence in God rather touchingly:

---

[16]   Ibid., 150.

[Hope] carries us forward in life. Someone will ask, "But how is this possible?" It is possible. It is possible if we cling to three firm convictions. First, God is all-powerful. Second, God loves me immensely. Third, God is faithful to His promises. Then once this trust has been kindled in me by Him, the merciful God, I no longer feel alone, or abandoned, or isolated; instead I feel myself involved in a plan of salvation which, carried out with the help of the Lord, will lead to the joy of heaven.[17]

"God is all-powerful. . . . God loves me immensely. . . . God is faithful to His promises." Or, we might put it another way: "God can do it. God wants to do it. God said he would do it." This is the content of our faith, and also the reason for our hope, and the theological virtue of hope trains us to keep our heart and mind fixed on these truths—attached to these "firm convictions," as the pope said. Caryll Houselander's insight is that by fighting our fears rather than accepting the situation that is making us afraid, we are taking our eyes and our minds off of the only thing that can really do anything to soothe our fears. Once we stop fighting, once we learn to drop our defenses and give up trying to solve every problem and escape every trial, we can finally become aware of just how close God is to us in the midst of our trials and how great is the love

17   John Paul I, General Audience of 20 September 1978. Quoted in *The Smiling Pope: The Life and Teaching of John Paul I*, trans. and ed. Raymond and Lauretta Seabeck (Huntingdon, IN: Our Sunday Visitor, 2004), 104–5.

WE DARE TO STRUGGLE 133

that he is offering to us. "'Without Me,' says Our Lord, 'you can do nothing.' That is often the first thing to realize when we are frightened, but often we remain unaware of His presence by being too much aware of our own."[18]

This is the central paradox for every disciple—that to become more fully ourselves, we must become more fully submissive to God's will and to his action in our lives. Perhaps no one was more acutely aware of this than Saint Paul, who describes his experience of handing himself over to God in quite frank terms in his second letter to the Corinthians (2 Cor 12:7–10). Throughout the time that he was an apostle, Paul had been blessed with mystical visions and revelations from the Lord. He also experienced great persecution, as well as a personal suffering which he calls "a thorn in the flesh" and "an angel of Satan" (2 Cor 12:7). He saw this challenging reality—which he does not describe in detail—as a just counterbalance to the blessings he had received, something that would keep him humble and prevent him from becoming conceited. It is not possible to say for certain whether the "thorn in the flesh" was a physical illness, or a severe temptation, or some other harassing suffering. What we do know for sure is that it bothered Saint Paul a great deal.

We can tell this because he admits that "three times I begged the Lord about this, that it might leave me" (2 Cor 12:8). Now, Saint Paul was a tough guy, used to roughing it and having to put up with lots of trouble along his way. He was no stranger to doing penance, and from his

---

18   Caryll Houselander, *The Comforting of Christ* (New York: Sheed and Ward, 1947), 148–50.

other letters, we know that he saw the value in bearing sufferings patiently for the sake of Christ and the Church. For him to pray so vehemently to be rid of this particular struggle, it must have been difficult indeed.

The Lord, however, did not answer this prayer in the way that Saint Paul hoped. He did answer him, but the answer was a clear "No." Still, there was more to the answer than that. The Lord told Paul, "My grace is sufficient for you, for power is made perfect in weakness" (2 Cor 12:9). The answer for Paul was not to get rid of the "thorn in the flesh" altogether, nor to try to face it all on his own with his own power, but to let the Lord's power work in him in the midst of his weakness. When Saint Paul realized this, his attitude changed: he began, he says, even to take joy in his weakness, because they were the reason "that the power of Christ may dwell with me" (2 Cor 12:9).

Theological hope allows us to recognize God as the source of our strength and to trust in his constant help. The more that we become mindful and aware of his ability and willingness to come to the aid of our weakness, the easier it becomes for us to admit and accept our neediness and even our fears and to admit with Saint Paul that "when I am weak, then I am strong" (2 Cor 12:10), because we realize that to acknowledge our weaknesses is the necessary first step to sharing in God's strength. Saint Paul came to this understanding through a direct communication from the Lord, after repeated prayer. Caryll Houselander reached a similar insight in the midst of a terrifying situation when she ran out of options and didn't know what else to do than to simply *be* terrified. Next, we are going to hear about a priest whose path to relying on God took a rather different and more frightening route—who, in fact, found himself in the darkness of despair before he was able to turn again to the light of God's love.

Total Surrender to God's Will—Father Walter Ciszek, SJ

One of the great joys of being Catholic is our faith in what we call the "communion of saints." Because the Lord Jesus calls his disciples to live in communion, not only with himself, but also with one another, there is a great exchange of charity, wisdom, and intercession among Christians, living and dead, around the world and across the centuries. I mentioned previously the way that the Apostles, for example, do and say things in the Scripture that allow us to learn from their example—they receive the answers (and sometimes the correction) from the Lord that we would like to have in their place. In a similar way, as we have been discussing the lives of these "heroes of hope," we benefit from the fact that the wisdom of these holy men and women was often acquired during moments of personal crises. They have endured the suffering alone with God, but they share the fruits of their experience with us. The next hero of hope we have to consider, the most modern of those we have talked about so far, also endured the most brutal suffering—so much so that most of his contemporaries gave him up for dead.

Walter Ciszek was born in Shenandoah, Pennsylvania, about one hundred miles northeast of Philadelphia, on November 4, 1904. The son of Polish peasants who had immigrated to the coal regions of Pennsylvania in the early 1890s, by all accounts Walter was a tough, street-fighting kid, whose father once asked the police to put him in reform school for his own good. Mr. Ciszek was as surprised as anyone in town when, in eighth grade, young Walter announced that he had decided to become a priest. He was sent to Orchard Lake, Michigan, to begin his seminary studies in a "minor seminary" program for high school-aged Polish students.

As a seminarian, Walter was determined to prove how tough he could be. "I'd get up at four-thirty in the morning," he recalled, "to run five miles around the lake . . . or go swimming in November when the lake was little better than frozen. I still couldn't stand to think that anyone could do something I couldn't do."[19] He imposed strict penances on himself—once going a whole Lent on bread and water, another time going for a whole year without eating meat—"just to see if [he] could do it,"[20] although he stayed up late at night to say his prayers in the chapel in private so that his fellow students wouldn't think that he was particularly pious.

In the seminary, Walter read the life of Saint Stanislaus Kostka, another tough Polish young man, who in the sixteenth century walked over 1,100 miles from Warsaw to Rome to join the newly-formed Society of Jesus—the Jesuits—despite the objections of his family. Walter was deeply impressed by the life of Saint Stanislaus and felt a

---

[19]   Walter Ciszek, *With God in Russia* (San Francisco: Ignatius, 1964), 20.

[20]   Ibid.

certain pull toward the Jesuits, although he resisted it at first, not wanting to leave Orchard Lake and have to begin again at a new seminary. When he finally decided, at the age of twenty-four, that he wanted to be a Jesuit, he simply took the train to New York, without telling anyone about it, and presented himself to the Jesuit provincial. After a rocky start, and over the protests of his father, Walter was accepted into the Society and was ordained a priest on June 24, 1937.

Early in his novitiate, in 1929, Walter and other Jesuit novices were read a letter from Pope Pius XI, appealing for seminarians from around the world who would volunteer to train for service in the missions in the Soviet Union. Listening to the pope describe life under the atheistic Communist regime, Walter was immediately convinced that this was what God was calling him to do, and as soon as the conference ended, he approached his superiors to tell them so. They encouraged him to think it over, and told him that, in any case, he would have to finish his initial formation before he would be ready to go to Rome to study. Walter persisted in his requests during his novitiate and his philosophy studies, and in 1934, he was sent to the newly-formed Russian College in Rome, where he studied language and liturgy for the next three years.

Following his ordination, Father Walter and some of his classmates were sent to serve in Poland since they could not travel directly into Russia. He spent two years in the town of Albertyn teaching Jesuit seminarians and ministering to the local Catholic community until the Nazi invasion on September 1, 1939 and the outbreak of

World War II. When the Soviets invaded from the east and occupied the area, they forced Father Walter to close his mission. With the permission of the Ukrainian Catholic archbishop of Lvov, Metropolitan Andrew Sheptytzky, Father Ciszek crossed the border into the Soviet Union in March 1940 under an assumed identity and began carrying out his priestly ministry secretly while working in the logging industry.

Father Ciszek was arrested in June 1941 and passed through a series of Soviet prisons for interrogation. Eventually he arrived at the notorious Lubyanka prison in Moscow, which was operated by the NKVD (the predecessor of the KGB), where he realized that the Soviets had discovered his true identity and that they were accusing him of spying for the Vatican. He was held at Lubyanka in almost continuous solitary confinement for nearly five years, during which time he was subjected to incessant interrogation and repeated torture of various kinds. After a particularly intense period of manipulation by a skilled interrogator, including drugging by a man who seemed to be a medical doctor, Father Ciszek signed a false confession and was convicted of espionage.

He was sentenced to fifteen years hard labor in Siberian labor camps in the Krasnoyarsk region and was eventually sent to Norilsk, two hundred miles north of the Arctic Circle, where winter temperatures reached 40 degrees below zero. There he worked in coal mines and processing plants by day and ministered clandestinely to his fellow prisoners along with other priests in the camp, facing not only physical hardships but the constant threat of being turned in by informants and subjected to further punishment or execution. After serving nine years, Father Ciszek was released and required to live under close supervision in Russia. His family and fellow Jesuits had presumed that he was dead, until he was given permission to write to his sisters in 1955. In October 1963, he was returned to the United States in an orchestrated exchange for a Soviet agent. He spent his remaining years giving talks and retreats through the John XXIII Center at Fordham University until his death on December 8, 1984.

Father Ciszek would stay another four years in Lubyanka after he had made the false confession that he thought might win his release. During this time, his captors continually tried to recruit him for "missions" to collaborate with the Soviets, offering to send him as a chaplain with a Red Army unit or to set him up in a Russian parish, from which he would report back to them, or even to send him back to Rome as a spy for the NKVD. Again and again, he resisted these attempts to manipulate him, but over time, both Father Ciszek and his captors grew weary with the process. The Soviet agents wanted an answer and continued to hint at their ability to punish him further, even to execute him, if he failed to cooperate. Father Ciszek, still ashamed of his false confession, and terrified that he might give in again, wondered if being executed might be such a bad thing, for it would put an end to the continual cat-and-mouse of the interrogations of Lubyanka. He found himself becoming overwhelmed by such thoughts, and suddenly a moment of crisis came upon him that would change his life forever. He describes it in his spiritual autobiography, *He Leadeth Me*:

> One day the blackness closed in around me completely. Perhaps it was brought on by exhaustion, but I reached a point of despair. I was overwhelmed by the hopelessness of my situation. I knew that I was approaching the end of my ability to postpone a decision. I could see no way out of it. . . . I saw only my own weakness and helplessness to choose either position open to me, cooperation or execution. . . .
>
> I don't really know how to put that moment in words. I'm not sure, even, how long that moment lasted. But I know that when it passed, I was horrified and bewildered; I knew that I had gone beyond all bounds, had crossed over the brink into a fit of blackness I had never known before. . . . I had been afraid before, but now I was afraid of myself. I knew I had failed before, but this was the ultimate failure. This was despair.[21]

By this time, Father Ciszek had been in prison for several years and had been through torture and great pain. He had been frightened and faced moments where he had felt lonely and abandoned, even desperate many times. But this moment had a new quality to it, which made it unlike anything he had ever encountered. This moment, he says,

---

[21]	Walter J. Ciszek, *He Leadeth Me* (San Francisco: Ignatius, 1973), 75.

was real despair. What made it different? Why did he lose hope?

For that is the definition of despair, as we have already seen: the decision, the choice of the will that refuses to accept God's help to keep moving forward. Despair says, "This is it. Here I stop. Nothing can change. God cannot do anything for me, and I will do nothing more." Father Ciszek is brutally honest about the reasons for his despair: in the midst of his loneliness and exhaustion, he admits, he had convinced himself that he was completely alone and "I had not even thought of or recalled the one thing that had been my constant guide, my only source of consolation in all other failures, my ultimate recourse: I had lost the sight of God."[22]

Here we can see clearly the difference that hope makes in the midst of loneliness and fear. For Father Ciszek is not the only one to have found himself in a crisis situation—on the edge of a knife, as it were, and able to go in either direction—and other "heroes of hope" whom we have encountered have chosen a different path. Matt Talbot, for example, came to realize all at once, on the street corner by O'Meara's Pub, that none of his so-called friends cared a whit for him when he was down on his luck and that he was completely alone. He could have taken this bitter truth, which "cut him to the heart," as a reason to sink first into self-pity and then into self-indulgence. Instead, hope led him to look to God for real friendship and for the strength to change his life. And Caryll Houselander, as we have seen, was able to hope in God's presence in the face

---

[22]   Ibid.

of the most frightening situations precisely because she *was* frightened and did not try to hide or fight it. Fear and loneliness need not lead to despair if, hoping, we keep our eyes on God instead of solely on ourselves.

Fortunately, this moment of despair did not last long for Father Ciszek. Rather, coming face to face with how far he had gone from God was just the jolt he needed to run back to him: "Recognizing that, I turned immediately to prayer in fear and trembling. I knew I had to seek immediately the God I had forgotten. I had to ask that that moment of despair had not made me unworthy of his help. I had to pray that he would never again let me fail to remember him and trust in him. I pleaded my helplessness to face the future without him. I told him that my own abilities were now bankrupt and he was my only hope."[23]

Father Ciszek recalls that, at this moment, and very suddenly, his heart was filled with consolation at the thought of Jesus and his agony in the Garden of Gethsemane. He began to realize, he writes, that there in the garden, in the midst of his suffering and in the face of his impending passion and death, the Lord Jesus knew the feelings of fear and human weakness that Father Ciszek himself was now experiencing. By meditating on the Lord's agony, Father Ciszek saw the way forward: as we have already seen, the way to deal with these very real fears and weaknesses was not to try to fight them alone, nor to simply wish them away. No: the lesson of the garden is that submission to the Father's will—"Not my will but yours be done"—leads to total self-surrender, and this hopeful

---

[23]   Ibid., 75–76.

handing over of self means handing over fears to God as well. Because God is omnipotent, he is able to handle our fears. Because, in the Incarnation, God has become Man, he is also able to understand them.

Father Ciszek described this moment of understanding as one that changed his life "from that moment on. I knew immediately what I must do, what I would do, and somehow I knew that I could do it. I knew that I must abandon myself entirely to the will of the Father and live from now on in this spirit of self-abandonment to God. And I did it. . . . It is all too simply said, yet that one decision has affected every subsequent moment of my life. I have to call it a conversion."[24]

We must not underestimate just what this meant for Father Ciszek, this complete self-surrender. From a certain perspective, perhaps it seems rather obvious: after all, by this time he has spent nearly five years in prison and has another nine years in Siberia awaiting him. Superficially, it seems that he has really very little choice but to depend on God; is it really such a great thing for him to profess total surrender when he's hit rock bottom? But we have to remember that this is the self-professed "tough" who, since childhood, always liked to have things his own way. This is the seminarian who never wanted to let anyone do anything he couldn't do; the priest who called his own shots as much as possible, even within his vow of obedience. This is the man who stood up to the KGB on a daily basis, and to this point had won the battle of wills. To surrender to this extent doesn't seem to have come

---

[24]   Ibid., 76.

naturally for Walter Ciszek, and he says as much as he describes what this moment of conversion meant to him:

> I had always trusted in God. I had always tried to find his will, to see his providence at work. . . . [But] up to this time, I had retained in my own hands the reins of all decision, actions, and endeavors. . . . I remained . . . in essence the master of my own destiny. . . .
>
> I had talked of finding and doing his will, but never in the sense of totally giving up my own will. I had talked of trusting him, indeed I truly had trusted him, but never in the sense of abandoning all other sources of support and relying on his grace alone. I could never find it in me, before, to give up self completely. There were always boundaries beyond which I would not go, little hedges marking out what I knew in the depths of my being was a point of no return. . . . I had trusted [God], I had cooperated with his grace—but only up to a point. Only when I had reached a point of total bankruptcy of my own powers had I at last surrendered. That moment, that experience, completely changed me.[25]

Once he experienced the power of God at work in his life, in all of the daily trials and situations that came his way, Father Ciszek was able to hope with absolute trust that he would be able to attain his goal of serving God and reaching eternal life. He was certain that God's power

---

[25]   Ibid., 76–77, 78.

would sustain him because he was equally certain that he had no real power of his own. Once again, we see the nature of theological hope as a *virtue*—because it is a habitual tendency, it's something that we've got to put into practice. The first act of hope can be a terribly difficult one to make if it has to be done in the midst of fear and struggle, or even in the face of despair. But when, with God's help, Father Ciszek was able to make the first act of hope and take down the obstacles that were keeping him from trusting in God completely, then the next act of trust and surrender came more easily. Hope built on hope:

> Across that threshold [that] I had been afraid to cross, things suddenly seemed so very simple. There was but a single vision, God, who was all in all; there was but one will that directed all things, God's will. I had only to see it, to discern it in every circumstance in which I found myself, and let myself be ruled by it.
>
> I looked no longer to self to guide me, relied on it no longer in any way, so it could not again fail me. . . . I was freed thereby from anxiety and worry, from every tension, and could float serenely upon the tide of God's sustaining providence in perfect peace of soul. . . . Secure in his grace, I felt capable of facing every situation and meeting every challenge; whatever he chose to send me in the future, I would accept.[26]

---

26   Ibid., 79–80.

The entire tone of Father Ciszek's spiritual autobiography changes after this incident: it becomes, in every sense of the word, a story of hope. The thing is, his struggles did not come to an end with this moment of his conversion; far from it, in fact. The interrogators still tried to cajole him into working with them, but Father Walter now calmly played along without committing to a thing because he knew that God would make sure his will was done. The day he finally left Lubianka, his captors told him it was to face a firing squad, and Father Walter went with a smile on his face, not because he wished for death, but because he knew that nothing could happen unless God willed it. He was taken, not to execution, but to the train depot, for the interminable trip in boxcars to Norilsk and nine years of hard labor in the mines and the refineries. There he faced daily threats—hardships from the living conditions; the cruelty of the guards; the worse treachery of fellow prisoners who acted as informants and were on the lookout for "subversive" activities—and even, once, faced the firing squad with which he had originally been threatened. Yet, despite the hardships, he worked diligently each day, and despite the danger of discovery, he and other priest captives carried out their ministry in secret to serve the needs of Catholics and others in the camp.

The virtue of hope had taken root in Father Ciszek's heart and soul that day in a marvelous way—in perhaps the only way it really could have done. There is an old Rabbinical story in which a young student asks the teacher, "Master, why does the Lord say to the prophet, 'I will write my laws on their hearts' (Jer 31:33)? Why does he not say, 'I will write my laws *in* their hearts'?" The master responds, "My son, the hearts of men are hard. The Lord can only place his words *on* their hearts and wait for the hearts of men to be broken by suffering. When their hearts are broken, then his words will enter into their hearts." Father Walter's heart was broken by despair that day in Lubianka. By God's providence, that moment of heartbreak became a new beginning for him—an opportunity to welcome grace and to begin exercising the virtues with renewed vigor. It is a testimony to his holiness that once Father Ciszek began living this way of hope, he didn't stop: from this point on, every day, every choice, his entire life belonged to God, and he would trustingly follow the path that God had set out for him, wherever it would lead.

5

We Dare to Suffer

Suffering Together With Christ—The Saints of Molokai

We have had a chance to discuss the ways in which
the virtue of hope teaches us to trust in God's providence and to look for his help in the midst of difficult
situations. Admittedly, the circumstances in which our
heroes of hope found themselves were not things that we
will have to face—God willing—but the lessons learned
and shared with us are applicable to all of our trials, large
and small.

There is a certain kind of trial that everyone faces at
some point in life in which this virtue becomes especially
important but which has a special kind of power to put
our hope to the test, and sometimes to stretch it to the
breaking point. I'm speaking, of course, of illness, which
afflicts nearly everyone personally in large or small ways
in his or her own bodies and—what is sometimes more
difficult to bear—also affects the ones we love.

Why does it become so difficult to trust God's providence

and love in the midst of illness? I think there are at least two reasons for this. One is that we are, simply put, just not *made* for it. The Catechism reminds us that according to God's original plan, human beings were created perfectly good: the human body was in perfect harmony with the human soul, with the natural world, and with God's plan. As long as that harmony remained intact, the human being would never have suffered, and would never have died.[1] Illness and death are tragedies that are connected with the deep mystery of sin, and we encounter them in this way; the fact that we find them distressing and even repulsive simply means that our perception and our consciences are working.

The virtue of hope assists us at this point to stay focused on the truth that the power of Jesus to redeem the world by his passion, death, and resurrection has overcome every evil, including sickness, suffering, and even death itself. Although we may experience individual incidents of suffering as powerful, even overwhelming tragedies, hope reminds us that the saving power of Christ is infinitely greater than any illness, that, as the Psalmist says, "The LORD sustains him on his sickbed . . . whenever he is ill" (Ps 41:4).

Another reason that sickness in particular causes such great distress, and in turn can lead a person to lose hope, is the reality that illness is by its nature *isolating*. When a person is sick and in physical pain, this sets him or her apart to a certain degree from family members and neighbors who are well and thus able to go about their regular

---

[1]   See CCC 376.

duties. This can lead to further pain and suffering—loneliness, thoughts that others do not understand or care, feelings of uselessness and worthlessness, and untold other distressing burdens. Ultimately, the emotional toll caused by the isolation—itself connected with the mystery of sin which divides human communities—becomes an even greater burden than the physical illness which first caused the pain. The Catechism insightfully warns that if it goes unchecked, this way of thinking "can lead to anguish, self-absorption, sometimes even despair and revolt against God."[2]

This is just that kind of desperate situation for which we have been given the theological virtue of hope to make it possible—because of God's power and initiative, not our own—to trust God when we need to the most. And although it seems like something we should get struck by lightning for suggesting—that the omnipotent Creator of the universe should have to prove himself to us poor creatures of dust and ashes—all of salvation history has been an ongoing process of God proving to human beings that he is, in fact, utterly trustworthy. At no time did he do this more explicitly or more convincingly than during the public ministry of the incarnate Son of God, when the Word became Flesh in order to show us exactly how much God loves the world.

From the beginning of his public ministry, Jesus Christ went about throughout Galilee and Judea working miraculous signs, including healing many people who were sick (see Mt 4:23–25; Mk 1:32–34; Lk 6:17–19). "Christ's

---

[2]   CCC 1502.

compassion toward the sick," the Catechism insists, "and his many healings of every kind of infirmity are a resplendent sign that 'God has visited his people' (Lk 7:16) and that the Kingdom of God is close at hand."[3] Lest the isolating effects of illness make us think that God had forgotten about us, the Lord Jesus identifies with us, particularly in our weaknesses.

One account of his healing ministry bears this out beautifully. After he had spent an entire evening, night, and early morning healing nearly the whole city of Capernaum at the home of Simon Peter and had sneaked out at dawn to try to get a few moments to himself for quiet prayer, he and his apostles were leaving town to move on to his next preaching stop. He was met unexpectedly by a leper who, knowing that he was responsible for letting people know he was "unclean" according to the law, presumably stood at a distance and simply said to Jesus, "If you wish, you can make me clean" (Mk 1:40). Much to everyone's surprise, Jesus reached out and touched the man, saying, "I do will it. Be made clean" (v. 41).

Jesus could have healed the man with a simple word, as indeed he did many times in the Gospels. But, because of his compassion, as Mark tells us, he deliberately extended his hands and made contact with this man, who had been isolated from all human contact for so long because of his infirmity. In doing so, he not only restored the leper to health but also reintegrated him into the community—and this came about by an action that would have made *Jesus,* in the eyes of the religious authorities at least, ritually

---

[3]   CCC 1503.

unclean. As he would do in a most perfect way on the Cross, the Lord takes away the leper's burden by taking it upon himself.

All disciples are called to imitate the self-sacrificing love that the Lord displays in this miraculous moment, but few have practiced it to the degree that we can see it in the life of the man who was chosen in 2005 as *De Grootste Belg,* the greatest Belgian of all time. The fourth son and seventh child of Frans and Anne-Catherine de Veuster, little Jozef, or "Jef" as he was called, was born in Tremelo, Belgium on January 3, 1840. Like two of his sisters and his brother Auguste, he became a religious in the Congregation of the Sacred Hearts of Jesus and Mary, a missionary community of priests, brothers, and nuns which had been founded in France at the time of the French Revolution. When he professed his vows on October 7, 1860, he took the name Brother Damien, presumably after Saint Damian of Cilicia, the twin brother of Saint Cosmas. Perhaps it seemed an appropriate choice for Jozef since his brother, Auguste, was already serving in the order; little did he know at the time how appropriate his choice of this patron saint—a physician who served the poor free of charge—would become later in his life.

Every day in the seminary, Damian would pray before a picture of Saint Francis Xavier, the patron saint of missionaries, that he would be considered worthy to be ordained and to be sent to the missions; eventually his prayer was answered when, in 1864, he was sent to Hawaii in place of his brother, who had been scheduled to go. Damien landed at Honolulu Harbor on March 19, 1864 and was ordained a priest at the cathedral there two days later. Over the next decade, he served in several parishes on Hawaii, "the big island," and on the island of Oahu.

During this time, the Kingdom of Hawaii (which was a sovereign nation from 1810 to 1893) was undergoing a crisis. The arrival of European explorers and traders in the eighteenth century brought many changes to the islands, not least of which was a number of diseases that the native Hawaiians had never encountered before. An outbreak of leprosy beginning in the early 1850s was devastating, not only for its debilitating effects on those who contracted it, but also for the fear that it inspired among the general population. At the time, as indeed throughout most of history, leprosy was thought to be highly contagious and incurable; we know now that it is transmitted by prolonged close contact through coughs and sneezes and that 95 percent of the population is naturally immune. Its appearance among the Hawaiian population caused a panic that led to drastic measures.

In 1865, the Hawaiian Legislature passed legislation establishing settlement colonies in which to quarantine victims of leprosy. These were to be at Kalaupapa and Kalawao on the eastern end of Molokai Island—a peninsula separated from the rest of the island by a steep mountain ridge and only accessible from the sea. "From that point on, leprosy became known as *Ma'i Ho'oka'awale,* "the separating sickness."[4] The Royal Board of Health

---

[4]   Jeanne Kun, "Apostle of the Lepers: The Life of Father Damian de Veuster of Molokai," *Living Bulwark,* vol. 34 (November 2009).

provided the quarantined people with supplies and food—about 140 of them were sent at first—and planned that they would be able to grow their own crops and survive as a small community on their own. However, they did not provide medical care or any training or guidance for leadership, and given the environment of the island and the condition of the sick, it was not long before chaos descended on Molokai.

The Catholic bishop of Hawaii, Louis Maigret, sent a priest to celebrate the sacraments on Molokai once a year, but he was reluctant to assign anyone to do more for fear of sending him to his death. In early 1873, the Catholics of Molokai sent a formal petition to him requesting a steadier arrangement; the bishop asked his priests to prayerfully consider whether they could volunteer for such a responsibility on a rotating basis three months at a time. Father Damian was the first to volunteer and arrived on Molokai on May 10, 1873.

Eight hundred sixteen lepers now resided on Molokai: six times as many as when it opened eight years before. Father Damian spent the night under a palm tree and got to work the next morning organizing the community as best he could. He tended the sick and dressed their wounds, built coffins for the dead and dug their graves. With the help of those who were well, he painted their crude shacks, built sturdy beds and then proper houses, and, in the center of things, constructed a parish church, which he dedicated to Saint Philomena. Under his influence, the lepers grew into a real community, with basic laws, a spirit of cooperation, and even working farms and organized schools. When it was time for the next priest in the "rotation" to take his turn, neither Father Damian nor the community wanted him to leave.

Thus, Saint Philomena's became Father Damian's parish, and the inhabitants of Molokai became his parishioners. He lived with them for nearly sixteen years all told and desired to give his whole heart and soul to the mission. About six months after his arrival on Molokai, he wrote a letter home to his brother Auguste; echoing the words of Saint Paul—"I have become all things to all, in order to save at least some" (1 Cor 9:22)—he wrote to his brother that "I make myself a leper with the lepers to gain all to Jesus Christ." At the time, perhaps, he was speaking only of sharing in their isolation, but eventually he would share in their illness as well.

The first sign came in December 1884 when, preparing for a bath, Father Damian accidentally put his foot into a vessel of near-boiling water. His skin was scalded and blistered, but he realized that he hadn't felt a thing—he had contracted leprosy and it was taking its toll on his skin and nerves. Some treatments eased his symptoms over the next few years, but he eventually succumbed to the disease on April 15, 1889 at the age of forty-nine. He was buried the next day under the same tree beneath which he had slept during his first night on Molokai.

Father Damian's reputation had spread quickly, especially after Princess Liliuokalani visited the island in 1881; when she returned, she shared her experiences with everyone she met, and the story of Father Damian's work soon spread throughout the United States and Europe.

However, it was difficult to find others who were willing to assist in the mission, although the need was great. In fact, more than fifty religious communities of women turned down a personal request from the king of Hawaii until he received an enthusiastic response from a Franciscan Sister from upstate New York named Mother Marianne Cope.

Barbara Koob was born on January 23, 1838 in Heppenheim, a medieval market town in southwestern Germany. Her family—her parents, four siblings, and herself—emigrated to the United States the following year and settled in Utica, New York; it was around this time that they began to spell their last name "Cope." Five more siblings were born in America. When Barbara was in eighth grade, her father became seriously ill; as the oldest of the children living at home, she needed to take work in a local factory to bring in money to support her parents and siblings.

Barbara's father died in 1862; by this time, her younger siblings were old enough to care for themselves, and she felt able to leave home and follow her vocation. She became a novice in the Sisters of the Third Franciscan Order of Syracuse, New York, and took the name Sister Marianne. On November 19, 1863 she professed her vows and served as a teacher and later as a principal in several schools in New York State. She soon displayed gifts for leadership and administration and was entrusted with the task of founding two of the first hospitals in central New York in the late 1860s—both of which were explicitly chartered to serve the sick without distinction as to a person's nationality, religion, or color, something unique for the time.

We can see the hand of Divine Providence in the decade or so that Sister Marianne spent in hospital ministry, as it prepared her for the day in 1883 when King Kalakaua's letter reached her desk. By this time, she was also serving the community as superior general and was known as Mother Marianne; it was up to her to oversee the assignment of her Sisters to ministries of all sorts. To her mind, nothing could be more pressing than the need of the lepers in Hawaii; she not only agreed to send her Sisters to take up the work but decided to go herself, confiding in the king that "I am hungry for the work and I wish with all my heart to be one of the chosen ones, whose privilege it will be, to sacrifice themselves for the salvation of the souls of the poor Islanders. . . . I am not afraid of any disease, hence it would be my greatest delight even to minister to the abandoned 'lepers.'"[5]

When they first arrived in Hawaii, the Sisters were given the task of caring for leprosy patients in the Kaka'ako Branch Hospital on Oahu Island. The branch hospital served as a first station for people from all of the islands; only the more severe cases were sent on to Molokai. After a year, Mother Marianne opened the Kapiolani Home nearby as a home for healthy girls whose parents had been stricken by leprosy—the first serious attempt made by anyone to take care of healthy children in close

[5]   "Bl. Marianne Cope (1838-1918)," http://www.vatican.va/ news_services/liturgy/saints/ns_lit_doc_20050514_molokai_ en.html, (1 March 2012).

proximity to their ill parents and to keep families together in some kind of unity.

A new government administration in 1887 took a hard line toward leprosy patients and enforced a stricter quarantine policy, closing the branch hospital on Oahu and sending everyone to Molokai. The authorities pleaded with Mother Marianne to move with her Sisters to the colony, and she did so immediately—"We will cheerfully accept the work," she said.[6] They were able to duplicate on Molokai the institutions they had run on Oahu and to take care of educating the girls living there. Mother Marianne was also able to offer spiritual comfort and nursing care to Father Damian, who was growing increasingly weaker as he succumbed to leprosy himself. She was by his side when he died in 1889 and was chosen to succeed him as the administrator of the boys' home on the island.

Mother Marianne continued to serve on Molokai for the next thirty years; she never contracted leprosy—a fact that some see as a sign of God's special favor and approval of her work and her sanctity—and died peacefully of natural causes on August 9, 1918 at the age of eighty. She had maintained contact with the hospitals and medical schools in Syracuse, as well as those on the other Hawaiian islands, and sponsored education and research programs aimed at finding new treatments and cures for those under her care. She also took an interest in the emotional and psychological well-being of patients that was exceptional.

---

[6]   *Saint Marianne Cope*, "Biography of Mother Marianne Cope – continued," saintmariannecope.org/biography3.html, (1 March 2012).

A nurse that worked on Molokai and took care of Mother Marianne in her last illness recalled in an interview many years later some of her insights:

> She revolutionized life on Molokai, brought cleanliness, pride and fun to the colony. People on Molokai laugh now—like other people in the world, laugh at the same things, the same dilemmas and jokes.
>
> It was Mother Marianne who bought the girls hair ribbons and pretty things to wear, dresses and scarves. Women keep their cottages and their rooms in the big communal houses neatly, pridefully. There are snowy bedspreads, pictures on the walls. They set their tables at meal time with taste, Mother Marianne brought that about.
>
> She interested the women in color harmony. Sit in services at the back of the church in Molokai and observe the lovely arrangements of color of the women. When Mother Marianne went to the island, people there had no thought for the graces of life. "We are lepers," they told her. "What does it matter?" Well, she changed all that. Doctors have said that her psychology was 50 years ahead of her time.[7]

We can see in the two saints of Molokai two approaches to fulfilling the same intention: bringing the love of Jesus Christ to those who are sick in order to overcome their

---

[7]   Sister Magdalene, quoted in *Saint Marianne Cope*, "Quotes of Note," saintmariannecope.org/quotes_note.html, (1 March 2012).

isolation. Father Damian went out to the lepers and lived among them to let them know that they did not suffer alone. Mother Marianne eventually joined him there; first and always she worked in large and small ways to keep families together and to give people pride in themselves, in their culture, and in their communities so that they would know that they *belonged* and that they were loved. Both of the saints of Molokai defended the human dignity of the lepers and loved them with that particular dimension of Christ's love called *compassion*, which means "to suffer with." In his encyclical on hope, Pope Benedict draws out another beautiful, important dimension of this love: "To accept the 'other' who suffers, means that I take up his suffering in such a way that it becomes mine also. Because it has now become a shared suffering, though, in which another person is present, this suffering is penetrated by the light of love. The Latin word *consolatio*, 'consolation', expresses this beautifully. It suggests being with the other in his solitude, so that it ceases to be solitude."[8]

As he reveals the secret of this consoling love, by which not only the saints but every disciple is called to "be with" those who are isolated, Pope Benedict admits that it is not always easy to love like this. We each have our own suffering to bear; it can be difficult to share the burdens of others as well. We won't be surprised at the solution that he offers—one on which Father Damian and Mother Marianne surely relied: "In all human suffering we are joined by one who experiences and carries that suffering with

---

[8]   Benedict XVI, *Spe Salvi*, 38.

us . . . and so the star of hope rises. . . . [The] capacity to suffer depends on the type and extent of the hope that we bear within us and build upon. The saints were able to make the great journey of human existence in the way that Christ had done before them, because they were brimming with great hope."[9]

Next, we're going to meet another of those saints brimming with hope, who was so radiant with joy that it shone out from her like a light and spread to everyone around her. They were convinced that her brilliant lamp was allowed to burn for far too short a time, but she would not let them be sad; on the contrary, those who went to cheer her up in the hospital found they usually had the tables turned on them, and she's been bringing people joy ever since.

Finding Joy in the Midst of Pain— Blessed Chiara Luce Badano

The virtue of hope became important in the home of our next hero long before she ever entered it. Ruggero Badano, a truck driver from Sassello in the Savona province of northeastern Italy, and his wife, Maria Teresa, had been happily married for eleven years by 1971, but they still prayed fervently that God would complete their joy and seal their love for one another with the blessing of children. When their daughter was born on October 29, they named her Chiara (the Italian form of the name Clare) and welcomed her as a true gift and an answer to their prayers. The long time that Ruggero and Teresa had spent hoping and trusting in God's plan gave them a perspective on

---

[9]   Ibid., 39.

their family's relationship with God and with one another that would become important in later years. "Right from the start," Teresa recalls, "we felt in our hearts that Chiara was not only our child, but first of all she was God's child, and as such, we had to bring her up respecting her freedom."[10]

Like Blessed Pier Giorgio Frassati two generations before her, Chiara Badano was a lively, energetic, outgoing child who brought great joy to her family and friends. Also like Pier Giorgio, she displayed a simple holiness and a generous concern for the needs of others from an early age. Her mother recalls one day when she came upon Chiara surrounded by some of her many toys. When Teresa suggested that they could easily give a few of them away to poor children who had none, Chiara instinctively clutched her favorites and ran off in tears to her room. A short time later, though, Teresa heard Chiara sorting out her toys into piles to keep and to give away—"This one yes, this one no!"—and soon the little four-year-old asked for a bag to pack up the toys for the poor. When Teresa looked in the bag, she was surprised to see that it was all of Chiara's new toys that she had chosen to donate. "Mamma," she insisted, "I cannot give old and broken toys to poor children!"[11]

Chiara also had a deep concern for those who were weak or sick and who were isolated from others as a result. As

---

[10]   *Chiara Luce: Life,* "The long-awaited arrival," http://www.chiarabadano.org/life/life/childhood/?lang=en, (Feb. 26, 2019).

[11]   Ibid.

a child, she would often visit the residents of the local retirement home, and as she got older, she loved to spend time with her grandparents, sometimes spending the night at their home to take care of them when they were ill. One Christmas, when her primary school class was sending letters to the Baby Jesus, she wrote to ask him, not for toys, but to make her grandmother and other sick people well in time to celebrate his birth. And when one of her classmates came down with chicken pox and other children were afraid to visit her, Chiara got her parents' permission to go and do her homework at this friend's house so that she wouldn't feel left out. "I think that love is more important than fear," she said.

When Chiara was just over nine, she met another girl a little older than herself on the train who soon became her best friend. This girl told her about a group called *Focolare*, a movement in the Church founded in the 1940s by Chiara Lubich, whose idea was to bring lay Catholics together for prayer, study, and good works in order to help them to grow in holiness and unity. Little Chiara was immediately taken with the idea of joining *Focolare*, especially when she heard about "Gen," a special "Third Generation" section that had been founded about ten years earlier specifically for youth between nine and sixteen years old.

As soon as Chiara got home, she told her parents about *Focolare* and Gen, and together they found out as much as they could about getting involved. She began writing to Chiara Lubich—a correspondence that would continue for the rest of her life—and read everything she could find about the way of life of this new movement. Chiara even convinced her parents to take her to "Familyfest," an international meeting of the families of the movement held in Rome in 1981, and the experience changed life for all three of them. Chiara was now fully committed to the idea that Jesus was calling her to become a saint, and she responded with a generous heart.

Home in Sassello, Chiara quickly became a leader among her circle of friends. Attractive and outgoing by nature, she was well-liked by lots of young people in the town, and many of them found themselves opening up and turning to her with their problems and doubts. They got together not only in church and formal meetings but in the tavern, at parties, on hiking trips, playing tennis, and swimming; they corresponded by postcard and kept in touch over the phone. Everyone found Chiara to be welcoming and a patient listener. At times her mother seemed to worry that Chiara was getting in over her head: that she would find it difficult to speak to people about God when she was just a young person, without formal theological training. Chiara reassured her: "I don't speak about Jesus; rather, I have to give him to them . . . by the way I listen to them, by the way I dress and above all, by the way I love them."[12]

The summer of 1988 was a happy one for Chiara. She was sixteen going on seventeen and was enjoying that rare pleasure: a normal, happy life. She was considering her future career and was toying with the idea of becoming a

---

[12]   *Chiara Luce: Life,* "Adolescence," www.chiarabadano.org/ life/life/adolescence/?lang=en, (1 March 2012).

flight attendant to indulge her spirit of adventure and have a chance to see the world. Then, during a tennis match that summer, she felt a sudden sharp pain in her shoulder. She didn't think much of it at first, and neither did her doctor. But the pain simply refused to go away. When, after several months, it was still there and getting worse, her doctor ordered tests. The following February, Chiara received the diagnosis: the pain was caused by osteogenic sarcoma, a particularly painful and deadly form of bone cancer that typically strikes children and youth. Chiara's case was well-advanced and had begun to spread.

Amazingly, Chiara took the news very calmly, courageously telling her parents, "I'm young, I'm sure I'll make it."[13] She underwent a serious surgery right away, with another one to follow in June. After the second surgery, the doctors were not hopeful; it was followed by frequent admissions to the hospital for chemotherapy treatments and other follow-up care. Chiara's family and friends came frequently to visit her, of course, thinking that they would have to cheer her up and lift her spirits in the midst of such a serious illness. But time and again, they were surprised to realize that it was she who taught them how to be joyful and how to accept the realities associated with her treatment with peace and trust.

In July 1989, Chiara's condition became even more serious: the spreading tumor caused an internal hemorrhage, leading to a loss of blood that nearly killed her. A blood transfusion saved her life and allowed another

---

[13]   *Chiara Luce: Life,* "Sickness," www.chiaraluce.org/Life_en/ Malattia_en, (1 March 2012).

year of life; however, around this time she also lost the use of her legs, and this year was spent completely confined to bed. Her chemotherapy meant that she was also losing her hair, of which she had always been so proud. But even these new challenges did not seem to faze her; as each brushful of hair came out, she would say, quietly but lovingly, "For you, Jesus."[14] With her family and her doctors, she decided to forgo further treatment against the cancer, which had become terminal, and to use only medications to prevent infections and alleviate her pain. But she declined to take the increasing doses of morphine that her physicians prescribed, saying that the drugs prevented her from thinking and praying clearly and that she wanted to be able to offer her sufferings consciously to Jesus.

In July 1990, when Chiara and her doctors decided that it was time to discontinue her cancer treatments, she wrote to Chiara Lubich to let her know what was happening. The founder of *Focolare*, who had become a kind of spiritual mother to her, wrote to console and encourage her and then gave a little gift that has inspired many people in the intervening years: "Chiara Luce is the name I have chosen for you," she wrote. "It is the light of God that conquers the world. I send it to you with all my love." *Chiara luce* in Italian means "clear light," and it was evident to everyone that saw Chiara Luce that the light of God's love was shining radiantly in her soul, even as the cancer was taking over her body.

Chiara Luce spent the remaining months at home with her parents, joined by a steady stream of visitors from

---

[14]   Ibid.

among the friends she had made in Gen 3 and her other connections in Sassello. She made sure that she was able to keep informed of the activities of the movement by phone and postcards, and even got her parents to set up a satellite dish so that she could watch Genfest '90, an international youth meeting held in Rome that summer. But it was clear to everyone that the day of her death was coming, and so, always the organizer, Chiara Luce worked with her mother to plan all the details for what she called her "wedding celebration"—her funeral. They picked the clothes in which she would be dressed, the music and the hymns, the readings for the Mass, even the flowers, and Chiara Luce insisted with her mother, "When you're getting me ready, Momma, you have to keep saying to yourself, 'Chiara Luce is now seeing Jesus.' . . . Don't shed any tears for me. I'm going to Jesus. At my funeral, I don't want people crying, but singing with all their hearts."[15]

On October 7, 1990, a priest from the *Focolare* movement arrived at the house and administered *Viaticum*, the sacrament of Holy Communion given as food for the journey from this world to the next. Chiara Luce spent the rest of the day praying at short intervals, "Come, Lord Jesus!" She died peacefully that evening, with her parents at her side and many friends in the adjoining room, just three weeks before her nineteenth birthday. Her last words, to her mother, were, "Goodbye. Be happy, because I'm happy."[16]

---

[15]   *Chiara Luce: Life,* "Departure," www.chiaraluce.org/Life_en/ Partenza_en, (1 March 2012).

[16]   *Chiara Luce: Life,* "Last times," http://www.chiarabadano.org/

It is clear to see that this story has the power to provoke deep emotions in anyone who hears it. Such a quick and painful death is always difficult to comprehend, but when suffering afflicts someone so vibrant, so generous, and so young—and, perhaps above all, so *innocent*—we feel the tragedy of it all even more deeply. It is all the more impressive when we consider with what grace and peace Chiara Luce seemed to bear up under all of her suffering. But sympathy for her, and anger at the apparent injustice of it all, may not be the only emotions that this story draws out of people. It is possible—we have to admit it—that some people hearing about Chiara Luce may have quite a different reaction. How could she just *take* it? They ask. How is it possible that someone just blindly accepts something so horrible without railing against it? And then, the question that really gets people angry—How can the Church hold someone so naïve up as an example to others? Do they really expect us to grin and bear it too?

These aren't *nice* questions, perhaps, but they're real, and they bear a close look, even if the people asking them don't always wait around for a real answer. Because if we understand Chiara Luce on her own terms, we see that she wasn't naïve at all and that her acceptance of God's will regarding her illness wasn't automatic. Rather, her coming to trust the Lord and his will was the result of a process, and if we understand how she did it, we can learn to do it as well.

Now, it's not possible to read Chiara Luce's mind, but in a way, we have the next best thing: the testimony of

life/life/last-times/?lang=en, (1 March 2012).

the people who knew her better than anyone else, her parents. Her mother describes Chiara Luce's moment of acceptance in a rather unique manner: "Chiara took twenty-five minutes to say her *yes* to God, and she never turned back."[17] Describing the day that Chiara came home from the meeting with her doctor when she received the diagnosis of cancer, Maria Teresa explains:

> I saw that she was walking very, very slowly. When she reached the door I asked her: Chiara, how did it go? Without looking at me, with a gloomy face, she answered: "Don't talk now," twice over, "Don't talk now." And she threw herself as she was on her bed.
>
> I wanted to tell her many things: *Don't worry. You are young.* But I had to respect her desire. I saw the huge struggle Chiara was facing within from her facial expression, because she knew that she had to say *yes* to Jesus, not only joyfully, but especially in suffering. But she couldn't manage because with the strength of a 17-year-old, she only wanted to live.
>
> After twenty-five minutes she turned towards me with her radiant smile as always, with a real gaze full of light, a wonderful smile, and said: "Mom, now you can talk," twice over, "Now you can talk."[18]

We have been discussing hope long enough by now that we don't have to do much guesswork to recognize

---

17   *Chiara Luce: Life,* "Illness," http://www.chiarabadano.org/life/life/illness/?lang=en, (1 March 2012).

18   Ibid.

what went on during those twenty-five minutes that Chiara Luce was in conversation with the Lord Jesus. It bears all the marks that we have come to recognize of exercising the theological virtue of hope. Chiara Luce does not avoid her real emotions but goes into her room taking all of her gloominess and struggles with her. Hope made it possible for her to put these trustingly in the hands of the Lord who understands them. Maria Teresa herself points out that this seventeen-year-old didn't have the strength to bear up under the burden by herself. Hope taught Chiara Luce to find her strength in the Lord and not in herself. The news she had received left her isolated, so much so that she could hardly talk, even to her own mother. Hope made her aware that with Christ to help her carry her cross, she was never, ever alone. She walked into her room weighed down by her diagnosis; she emerged buoyed up by hope.

That it is truly hope at work in Chiara Luce's heart can be seen in the transformation that takes place, not only in her attitude toward her illness, but in her outlook on life in general. Her father describes this as the moment "when a dramatic change took place in Chiara Luce's life and her rapid ascent towards holiness began"[19]—no small thing considering how good she had been up to this point. Theological hope allowed Chiara Luce to see the path that God had marked out for her and to commit herself to walking that path, even though it now seemed a great deal shorter than she had previously anticipated. If it was his path, his plan, she seems to be convinced, then all the details were his to work out, including the timing, and she adopted an

---

[19]   *Chiara Luce: Life,* "Sickness."

attitude of peaceful indifference and acceptance. "Jesus sent me this illness at the right moment,"[20] she wrote to a friend, and she made use of her stays in the hospital to console her fellow patients, and even her doctors. In hope, she came to see her life as a cooperative effort with Jesus—her path was his path, and so she did not complain. "For you, Jesus," she would say in the face of difficult treatments and painful moments. "If you want it, I want it too!"[21]

Her path was his path, she came to see with eyes of hope, and of course, his path was always the Way of the Cross, the way of suffering that leads inevitably to his passion, his cross, and his death. Because she saw this path with eyes of faith and hope, Chiara Luce was able to accept her own coming death with peace and serenity; moreover, she was even able to share this outlook with those around her. Doctor Antonio Delogu, one of her physicians, testifies to the impact that Chiara Luce's attitude had on him and others at the hospital. "Through her smile, and through her eyes full of light," he says, "she showed us that death doesn't exist; only life exists."[22] Because hope not only showed her the possibility of walking the Way of the Cross with Jesus but also the reward of the resurrection that lay at the end of it, Chiara Luce was able to see her sufferings in their proper light and to judge them in proportion to eternal life. "If I had to choose between walking or going

---

20   Ibid.

21   Ibid.

22   Ibid.

to heaven," she said in 1989 when she lost the use of her legs, "I would choose going to heaven."[23]

Saint Paul, who suffered himself in so many ways, had a similar insight, which he shared with the Romans: "I consider that the sufferings of this present time are as nothing compared with the glory to be revealed for us" (Rom 8:18). He put it even more emphatically in his second letter to the Church in Corinth: "We are not discouraged; rather, although our outer self is wasting away, our inner self is being renewed day by day. For this momentary light affliction is producing for us an eternal weight of glory beyond all comparison, as we look not to what is seen but to what is unseen; for what is seen is transitory, but what is unseen is eternal" (2 Cor 4:16–18).

"We are being renewed day by day." We mustn't let the idea that Chiara Luce's *yes* to the Lord, which came in "twenty-five minutes," lead us to think that that was all there was to it. Rather, having once made her commitment to follow the Lord, she needed to recommit herself day by day to keeping that commitment in the face of the ups and downs of her illness and all of the daily trials it would bring. She once confided in her mother that when the worst pains came, she sang in her heart a folk song she had learned as a little girl: "Here I am, O Jesus, today as well, I'm here before you."[24] *Today as well* . . . the words of someone "on the way," who has learned to make daily the acts of hope and trust in God's strength that keep her going.

---

23   Ibid.

24   Ibid.

Chiara Luce was beatified in September 2010, and her story of illness transformed by hope has become an inspiration for a whole generation of youth. Now we will learn about a woman whose heroic, hopeful suffering gave the gift of life to those whom she loved.

Suffering as a Gift—Saint Gianna Molla

Gianna Francesca Beretta was born in Magenta, Italy, a town in the Lombardy region of northern Italy, not far from Milan, on October 4, 1922. Her parents, Alberto and Maria Beretta, must have been delighted that her birthday fell on the feast of Saint Francis of Assisi: they were both members of the Franciscan Third Order; that is, they followed a modified form of the Rule of Saint Francis as they pursued their secular vocations and lived in the world. Gianna was the tenth of the thirteen children in her family, of whom nine survived to adulthood. Alberto and Maria made sure that all of their children received a solid education in the Catholic faith and took the whole family to daily Mass early each morning.

The Berettas were also concerned that their children—daughters as well as sons—would all study a profession so that they would be able to serve God and their neighbor and spread the Gospel in the world. Two of Gianna's brothers became engineers; like two other brothers and three of her sisters, Gianna decided to study medicine. During Gianna's last year of secondary school, however, her mother died of a sudden stroke and a heart attack at the end of April 1942; her father's death quickly followed on the first of September. These tragedies and the realities of

World War II caused some delays, but eventually Gianna was able to enroll in the University of Pavia, about half an hour from Milan, and she earned her doctorates in Medicine and Surgery in 1949. She had considered becoming a medical missionary in Brazil but gradually came to understand that she could live her vocation right where she was. She opened a medical clinic in Mesero, close to Magenta, in 1950, and in 1952, she was recognized as a specialist in pediatrics.

Since her high school days, Gianna had been inspired to get involved in "Catholic Action," a group for lay people that encouraged a more intensive spiritual life and active charitable and apostolic work. As she began to live her medical career, she came to see it more and more as her vocation, as a real service to God and to his people. She had specifically chosen the field of pediatrics because she thought that in that way, she could have the most influence on family life by having frequent contact with young mothers and a chance to talk with them on a regular basis and to help them through difficult moments in their lives. She listened patiently to the needs of her patients, and when she knew that their illnesses came from bad moral choices, she gently but firmly tried to help them return to the right path. She had a marvelous insight into the opportunity that her profession gave her to be part of people's lives:

> Everyone works in the service of man. We doctors work directly on man himself. . . . The great mystery of man is Jesus: "He who visits a sick person, helps

me," Jesus said. . . . Just as the priest can touch Jesus, so do we touch Jesus in the bodies of our patients. . . . We have opportunities to do good that the priest doesn't have. Our mission is not finished when medicines are no longer of use. We must bring the soul to God; our word has some authority . . . Catholic doctors are so necessary![25]

While visiting her brother's medical office in 1949, Gianna first met Pietro Molla, an engineer from Mesero. As it turned out, his family lived directly across the street from her own office, and the two had several fleeting encounters over the next few years which Pietro never forgot—but which don't seem to have made much of an impression on Gianna at the time. At any rate, in December 1954, a mutual friend who was being ordained a priest invited both of them to attend the celebration of his first solemn Mass; they ran into each other at the reception after the Mass and became reacquainted. They began to cross paths more frequently and then to make plans to see each other; by February 1955, Pietro was ready to propose marriage, and Gianna joyfully accepted. On March 7, Pietro wrote in his diary, "The more I know Gianna, the more I am convinced that God could not have given me a greater gift than her love and companionship."[26]

---

[25] *Saint Gianna Beretta Molla: Wife, Mother, Doctor, Prolife Witness*, "St Gianna's Life: Doctor," www.saintgianna.org/doctor.htm, (1 March 2012).

[26] *Saint Gianna Beretta Molla: Wife, Mother, Doctor, Prolife Witness*, "St Gianna's Life: Marriage Proposal," www.saintgianna.org/marriproposal.htm, (1 March 2012).

Pietro and Gianna were married on September 24, 1955, in the Basilica of Saint Martin in Magenta. They were quickly blessed with children: their son, Pierluigi, was born the following November. Two daughters would follow soon after: Maria Zita (always called Mariolina) in December 1957 and Laura in July 1959. A couple of weeks before their wedding, Gianna had written to Pietro and described what the idea of their one day becoming parents meant to her: "With God's help and blessing," she wrote, "we will do our best to make our new family a little Cenacle where Jesus reigns over all our affections, desires, and actions," referring to the Upper Room where the Blessed Mother prayed with the apostles after Jesus ascended into heaven. "We will become collaborators with God in His creation," she continued, "and so we will be able to give him children that love and serve him."[27] As an act of thanksgiving after each birth, Gianna took money from her savings—an amount equivalent to six months of a workman's salary—and donated it to the missions.

Pietro and Gianna were glad at the idea of having many children, as many as God might see fit to send them, and so they were overjoyed to find out in the summer of 1961 that Gianna was expecting another child. Several miscarriages had followed the birth of Laura, so a healthy baby on the way was an answer to prayer. Around the end of the second month of the pregnancy, however, an unexpected pain in the area of the uterus began to cause Gianna

---

[27]　*Saint Gianna Beretta Molla: Wife, Mother, Doctor, Prolife Witness*, "St Gianna's Life: Children," www.saintgianna.org/children.htm, (1 March 2012).

a great deal of concern. Her medical training told her to be wary; soon tests revealed the presence of a *fibroma*, a benign growth of connective tissue sometimes called a *fibroid* or a *fibroid tumor*, growing in her uterus.

Although the fibroma was not cancerous, to allow the growth to remain where it was in the uterus would have been increasingly painful for Gianna and dangerous for her baby, possibly leading to the development of fetal abnormalities or to a miscarriage. Medical science in the 1960s presented her with two morally permissible options: Doctors could perform a hysterectomy; that is, they could remove the entire uterus. This would, of course, end the life of the child she was carrying. Because the death of the unborn child would not be directly intended but only foreseen, it could, from a moral perspective, be accepted as an unintended bad effect of a good action—namely, the medical intervention to remove the tumor. This moral principle is known as the principle of "double effect" and applied in cases when there is a sufficiently grave reason to accept a bad consequence along with a good one.

The other, riskier option was to undergo surgery in order to remove the tumor while allowing the pregnancy to continue. This procedure would be more dangerous for both mother and child, as it would bring the risk of uncontrollable bleeding, as well as possible rupture of the uterus later on, especially at the time of delivery.

As a physician, Gianna was fully aware of her medical options and of all of the risks involved. As a Catholic, moreover, she knew that it would have been morally permissible to perform the safer hysterectomy. Nevertheless,

she made the heroic decision to accept the dangers associated with the fibroidectomy, and she pleaded with her
doctors to do the riskier surgery in order to save the life of
her child. She accepted the higher risks for herself in order
to provide a better opportunity for her baby.

When the baby came to term in late April, the doctors
tried to induce natural labor using oxytocin since Gianna's
previous surgery made a natural rather than surgical birth
the safer alternative. From the afternoon of April 20—
Good Friday that year—until about 10:00 the next morning, Gianna's physicians tried everything they could to
move labor along but finally decided that they need to proceed with a Caesarean section. Gianna knew from years of
pediatric and obstetric experience just what this entailed
with the state that her body was in. But she was very clear
with her surgeons on the way to the operating theater.
"If you must decide between me and the child," she told
them, "do not hesitate: I demand it, the child, save it."[28]

She underwent general anesthesia, and her third daughter, Gianna Emanuela, was born completely healthy not
long after, weighing in at nearly ten pounds. The elder
Gianna's condition began to decline almost immediately,
however, as she quickly developed a fever and a rapid,
weak pulse. Although doctors administered antibiotics,
septic peritonitis—an infection of the lining of the abdomen—spread quickly, almost certainly contracted during
the surgery which she had undergone in her already

---

[28]   *Saint Gianna Beretta Molla: Wife, Mother, Doctor, Prolife
       Witness*, "Medical Circumstances of Death," www.saintgianna.
       org/medicalcircum.htm, (1 March 2012).

weakened state. Gianna suffered greatly for a week, and amid great pain, she died on April 28, 1962 at the age of thirty-nine. As she was dying, she repeatedly cried out, "Jesus, I love you! Jesus, I love you!"

Even at her funeral Mass, the people of Gianna's parish noted their great love for her and their respect for her unique self-sacrifice by preparing a burial place for her in the crypt under the altar, where the parish priests were entombed. About a year later, a priest-friend of the family wrote and privately published a little pamphlet about her life and virtues; this was followed in 1970 by the approval of the diocesan bishop for a formal investigation into Gianna's life, with the idea of proposing her for canonization. Gianna was beatified by Pope John Paul II in 1994 during the International Year of the Family, and the same pope declared her a saint ten year later in the presence of her husband and of the daughter whom she gave her life to save.

It's important to make a few things clear when we're talking about the life, and the sacrifice, of Saint Gianna. First of all, the choice that she made regarding that first surgery, to take the more complicated and riskier option to remove the fibroid rather than the hysterectomy, was a personal one, and in many ways, a heroic one—and, as we have already seen, Gianna would have been justified in making a different choice. When we are evaluating moral choices, it is important to know clearly both *what* a person is doing—this is called the *object* of the act—and the *reason* a person is doing it—this is called the *intention*. If both the object and the intention are good, then the act is good; if either one is evil, then the act is evil—it is not permissible to do a good thing for a bad reason or to do evil so that good may come from it.

In Gianna's case, the *object* of the act—the thing she was considering doing—would not have been an abortion but rather a medically indicated intervention on an organ (the uterus) that had become diseased. This action, which is morally good, would have had two foreseeable effects, one good (sustaining her health) and one bad (ending the life of her child). It would have been justifiable to do this action and accept both the good and the bad effects, according to Catholic moral teaching, as long as her intention was good—that is, that she did not *want* to end the baby's life but merely accepted the reality that it would happen—and that the good effect was proportionate to the bad effect—in this case, that her life was also at stake.

I mention this because the choice that Gianna made was clearly not an easy one, and, more importantly, is not a choice that everyone in her situation would make. It is necessary for us to understand that the Church does not require or expect everyone faced with a similar choice to take the path that Saint Gianna chose; that in fact, to choose differently, provided that one's intentions are correct, is a morally permissible decision. It would not imply that one is any less virtuous, or even less charitable, if one were to act differently than Saint Gianna in such a case.

So, why *does* the Church hold Saint Gianna up as an example for all to imitate? Why *have* popes and bishops, mothers and fathers—all sorts of people in all sorts of circumstances—found in her an inspiration and a model?

What led Pope John Paul II to call her "an example of Christian perfection"[29] and a "significant messenger of divine love?"[30]

If we look closely at the life of Saint Gianna, what we find is that her willingness to give of herself did not begin when she went into the hospital to have labor induced on Good Friday 1962, nor when she discussed her plans for surgical options to deal with her fibroma with her physicians earlier that year, nor even when she found out she was expecting Gianna Emanuela. Her self-sacrificing love was evident in every one of the relationships that held her family together; it was growing and developing from the day she fell in love with Pietro and determined that building a family with him was truly her vocation.

Gianna's writings from around the time of her engagement show that she understood clearly what it meant to be called by God to a particular vocation:

> Everything has a specific end: everything obeys a law. God has shown each one of us the way, the vocation, and the life of grace that lies beyond physical life. Our earthly and eternal happiness depends on following our vocation without faltering.
>
> What is a vocation? It is a gift from God—it comes from God himself. Our concern then, should be to know the will of God. We should enter into the

---

[29]   John Paul II, Homily at the Beatification Mass of Blessed Gianna Molla et al., St Peter's Square, 24 April 1994.

[30]   John Paul II, Homily at the Canonization Mass of Saint Gianna Molla et al., St Peter's Square, 16 May 2004.

path that God wills for us, not by "forcing the door,"
but when God wills as God wills.[31]

Of course, we can recognize these words by now as
the voice of one who is exercising theological hope, who
sees the path that God has set for her and responds to it,
striving to walk along that road trusting in the strength and
help that comes from the Lord. Gianna certainly needed to
trust in God's plan for her and in his strength: with three
small children at home and a thriving medical practice
serving the poor of Mesero, she definitely had her hands
full, particularly on occasions when Pietro spent periods
away by himself in the mountains. But through it all,
Gianna maintained a hopeful confidence in God's timing
and God's judgment, reasoning that if he had a plan for her
life and her circumstances, then he had also determined
how to provide for all of her needs. "When one does one's
own duty," she said, "one must not be concerned, because
God's help will not be lacking. . . . God's providence is in
all things, it's always present."[32]

Thus, we can see that the great sacrifice that Gianna
made in the last months of her life—which we might mark
as beginning with her first surgery and ending with the
infection that caused her death—was simply the capstone,
the seal, on the constant, daily sacrifices that she made to
her family, and especially to her children. In a way, we

---

[31]   "St Gianna's Life: Marriage Proposal."

[32]   *Saint Gianna Beretta Molla: Wife, Mother, Doctor, Prolife
Witness*, "Reflections of St Gianna Beretta Molla," www.
saintgianna.org/reflections.pdf, (1 March 2012).

have to ask ourselves whether Saint Gianna would have seen any of this as something extraordinary; after all, she spoke often of doing her duty and was surrounded in her practice by many poor women, mothers who made what she considered far greater sacrifices than she on a daily basis in order to provide for the needs of their children. "Look at the mothers who truly love their children," she wrote on one occasion, "how many sacrifices they make for them. They are ready for everything, even to give their own blood so that their babies grow up good, healthy and strong."[33] Little did she know, perhaps, that this trait she so admired in other women was one she would embody herself.

Saint Gianna may not have considered her way of living or her way of loving heroic, but the popes certainly did. At the Mass for her beatification, Pope John Paul II said that Saint Gianna was a model for "all those high-spirited mothers of families who give themselves completely to their family . . . who are prepared for every kind of labor and every kind of sacrifice, so that the best they have can be given to others."[34] When he celebrated the canonization Mass a decade later, John Paul compared Saint Gianna to the Lord who loved his disciples "to the end" (Jn 13:1), saying that Gianna "remained heroically faithful" to her marriage vows by making an "extreme sacrifice she sealed with her life."[35]

---

[33] "Reflections of St Gianna Beretta Molla."

[34] John Paul II, Homily at the Beatification Mass of Blessed Gianna Molla et al., St Peter's Square, 24 April 1994.

[35] John Paul II, Homily at the Canonization Mass of Saint

Once again, the ability of Saint Gianna, and of any wife and mother—or husband and father, for that matter—to remain faithful to all the commitments that marriage and family life entails, to keep on loving "to the end," necessitates an active practice of the virtue of hope, which keeps us always "on the way," always moving toward the goal, never resting on our laurels as if the journey were over, but continually deepening our commitment to love as we are loved. Because Saint Gianna was full of hope, there was always room for new depths to her love. Because she was prepared in hope to give of herself—and in fact had been doing so in many ways for many years—her gift of her life was not an isolated incident but the culmination of a lifetime's worth of practice, of little, constant acts of hope and love.

"One earns Paradise with one's daily task," Saint Gianna once said.[36] Throughout her life, her hope that her path was leading, slowly but definitely, toward eternal life gave her the strength to keep moving along it with God's help, whatever twists and turns it might present to her. Saint Gianna's husband, Pietro, testified that the day after the Caesarean section, when her infection had struck and the beginning of the end had come, Saint Gianna received a special gift from God that strengthened her hope:

Gianna Molla et al., St Peter's Square, 16 May 2004.

[36] *Saint Gianna Beretta Molla: Wife, Mother, Doctor, Prolife Witness*, "Reflections of St Gianna Beretta Molla," www. saintgianna.org/reflections.pdf, (1 March 2012).

I still see Gianna when, on Easter morning in 1962 . . . she took the child in her arms with great effort. . . . From that day, her pain became constant. . . .

It seemed like a slow, dramatic sacrifice, accompanying that of Christ on the cross. Her suffering became even more intense on Monday. . . . During the night between Tuesday and Wednesday after Easter, her condition sharply worsened. Wednesday morning it took a temporary turn for the better and she told me "Pietro, I was on the other side already and if I could tell you what I saw! One day I will. But since we were too happy with our wonderful children, full of health and grace, with all of heaven's blessings, they sent me back here, to suffer more, because it is not right to knock at the Lord's door without having suffered greatly."

This was the last time I was able to speak with my wife. Afterwards, she said a few more words, but for me this was her testament of joy and suffering, of devotion and faith in God.

A glimpse of heaven, given by God's grace, gave Saint Gianna the ability to endure courageously the ten days or so that she still had to suffer on earth, which she faced with the attitude that since the Lord had made her so happy for so long on earth, she was more than willing to suffer with him for a little while longer before leaving the world to go to him.

In Saint Gianna we are confronted with a special kind of suffering: more deliberate, we might say, even more "voluntary" in a way, and therefore, seemingly, more "avoidable." Yet thus we come to realize just how very necessary is the virtue of hope if we are going to suffer well. It is natural for us, at least in our fallen human nature, to look for ways to avoid suffering and pain, but the Lord Jesus never does; on the contrary, he chooses to be with us when we suffer and embraces the Cross to save us from suffering and death. Hope trains and teaches us to remember and to imitate the model he had set for us and to rely on his strength and his compassion so that we may "suffer with" him and turn to him in all of our needs.

6

We Dare to Pray

Face to Face as Friends—Moses

Through the course of our book so far, we have encountered many "heroes of hope" who have gone through a wide variety of experiences in very diverse circumstances. Each of them, in their own particular way, shines a little bit of light on one or another facet of the theological virtue of hope that we have been working to understand and put into practice. For all of their diversity, though, all of our saintly models have one very important thing in common: they would never have been able to do anything at all without a relationship with almighty God, and that relationship would never have gone anywhere without communication—that is, without *prayer*. Now we are going to take a look at some of the ways that prayer is related to the virtue of hope and how hope can overcome some of the obstacles we encounter in prayer.

The first encounter we find between Moses and the Lord is a dramatic one indeed—one of the most memorable in all the Scriptures: As Moses is tending flocks of sheep for his father-in-law, Jethro, he comes to Mount Sinai. There, he sees a marvelous sight: a bush that is filled with fire, yet is not burned up. As he approaches to investigate, he hears a voice calling his name and telling him to remove the sandals from his feet because he is on holy ground; the voice identifies itself as the voice of God, "the God of Abraham, the God of Isaac, and the God of Jacob" (Ex 3:6), the ancestors of Moses's people.

The Lord continues to speak to Moses from the burning bush and tells him that he has seen the sufferings that his people are enduring in Egypt. He has heard their cry, the Lord says, and knows what they are going through, so he has come down to rescue them, and he has a plan. Then the Lord tells Moses that he must be the one to accomplish that plan: that it will be Moses who must stand before the Egyptian pharaoh and demand the release of the Israelites.

Even today we can grasp the grandeur and great mystery of this moment when the all-powerful God announced that he had taken such an intimate interest in the affairs of his Chosen People, that he had taken such a keen and personal interest in their suffering, and that he had come to set them free from their oppressors. But Moses's reaction to God's words to him from the burning bush were rather different from this. He balks at the suggestion almost immediately: "Who am I," he asks, "that I should go to Pharaoh?" (Ex 3:11). God promises that success won't depend on Moses's strength alone but that he will be with him in all of his endeavors. But Moses isn't finished with his protestations: *What if the people don't believe me? What should I say if they ask me who you are? You know that I can't speak very well. My brother Aaron speaks much better than I do: send him instead.* Time and again, Moses offers reasons to the Lord to suggest why he is not the right man for the job, and time and again the Lord answers with reassurance that he knows exactly what he is doing and has chosen correctly. Finally, Moses simply cries out, "If you please, my Lord, send someone else!" (Ex 4:13). Curiously, the Lord does not answer this final plea directly. The Scripture simply says that he was angry with Moses and sent him to go and do what he commanded him to do.

On the way home, he meets his brother Aaron, and they begin to discuss the experience that Moses has had and the word he received from the Lord about their mission. Together they go to gather the Israelite community to share the news with them as well; at first, they react with gratitude and faith and bow down in worship to the Lord who is coming to save them. Moses and Aaron next go to Pharaoh to deliver the Lord's message. Pharaoh responds that he's never heard of "the Lord," and even if he had, he would never let the Israelites leave his kingdom. He accuses Moses of inciting the people to be lazy about their work, and in retaliation, he increases their daily quota while reducing their work supplies. The representatives of the people come to Moses and Aaron and rebuke them, blaming them for causing the hardships they were now facing.

The book of Exodus tells us that "Moses again had recourse to the LORD" (Ex 5:22)—that is, he went back to pray to the Lord again. But his prayer was something we might not expect: "Lᴏʀᴅ," he says, "why have you treated this people badly? And why did you send me? From the time I went to Pharaoh to speak in your name, he had treated this people badly, and you have done nothing to rescue your people" (Ex 5:22–23). My life was a lot better before you got me into this, Moses seems to say. You've forgotten your people, and you haven't kept your promises.

What are we to make of a prayer like this one? Well, the way that we react to it will depend an awful lot on the attitude that we start with, on what we assume "good prayer" is "supposed" to sound like. If we are under the impression that prayer always has to be very organized, very pretty, very demure and pietistic, very polite and usually uttered in a whisper—well then, no, Moses's prayer certainly doesn't qualify. But the result of this prayer— of this fervent, animated pouring out of his heart to the Lord—was a renewal of God's promises to Moses and to his people. "Now you will see," the Lord said, "what I will do to Pharaoh. . . . I am the Lᴏʀᴅ. . . . I am mindful of my covenant" (Ex 6:1, 2, 5). Although it may be difficult for us to understand how Moses is able to pray as he does, the Lord certainly seems to accept it.

The entire fourth section of the *Catechism of the Catholic Church* is dedicated to a discussion of prayer, including a detailed analysis of the *Our Father*. First, though, it addresses a number of basic, introductory questions on the topic, including "Where does prayer come from?" In a very touching paragraph, the Catechism explains:

"Whether prayer is expressed in words or gestures, it is the whole man who prays. But in naming the source of prayer, Scripture speaks sometimes of the soul or the spirit, but most often of the heart (more than a thousand times). According to Scripture, it is the heart that prays. If our heart is far from God, the words of prayer are in vain."[1]

Here, I think, is the explanation to how Moses' prayer, as blunt and jarring as it might seem to some people, could undoubtedly be pleasing to God. Prayer is communication with God, and if communication is not honest, then it is not communication at all. If Moses was going to pray, if he was *really* going to pray, really going to communicate with the living God whom he had encountered, then he needed to say what was in his heart and on his mind— say it with honesty, say it as it needed to be said—or it would have been better for him not to "pray" at all. In this instance, as in his argument with the Lord over his mission—on Mount Sinai on the day of the burning bush— Moses is speaking intimately, and therefore honestly, with God.

The Catechism sees a connection between these two incidents—such that the experience that Moses had that day on Sinai actually taught him how to communicate honestly with God: "Only after long debate does Moses attune his own will to that of the Savior God. But in the dialogue in which God confides in him, Moses also learns how to pray: he balks, makes excuses, above all questions: and it is in response to his question that the Lord confides

---

[1]   CCC 2562.

his ineffable name, which will be revealed through his mighty deeds."[2]

Here we can see the virtue of hope at work, as Moses discerns the call that comes to him directly from God. This is, of course, a somewhat different process of discernment than we were discussing earlier; here, it is not so much a question of what God wants—that is very clear!—but of whether Moses can respond to it. And that, at first, seems clear as well: as far as Moses is concerned, the initial answer is "no." But the virtue of hope draws something in him to continue the conversation: it keeps his heart and mind fixed on the fact that God has a plan for him and that he ought to respond to it, even though he finds it difficult to do so. Otherwise, why doesn't he simply walk away? Instead, he debates with the Lord, and at each stage in the argument, God answers him with reasons for hope. I don't think the people will believe me, Moses says. I'm telling you my Name so you can call on me, the Lord tells him. I *know* Pharaoh won't listen to me, Moses counters. I will be with you, and I will work signs for you to show him, says the Lord. I'm not strong enough, talented enough, smart enough, smooth enough; send someone else. I know all that already, the Lord seems to say, and anyway you don't have to be any of those things; I will be your strength, so stick with me.

This formative conversation at the burning bush taught Moses to rely on the Lord—it became the source of and reason for his hope and allowed him to pray hopefully in difficult situations. It is also the reason that he can pray

---

[2]   CCC 2575.

rather pointedly in situations like the one we've just discussed, where it seems to him that the Lord isn't keeping
his promises. Moses "agreed"—well, I suppose he agreed
. . . at least he stopped resisting—to take on this mission
because the Lord promised to be with him. To pray in this
way does not imply a doubt on his part; far from it . . . it
shows, I think, how much he truly does believe and hope
in the Lord's promises: enough to call the Lord on it if he
perceives that the Lord is slow in fulfilling them.

The Catechism says that as "the promise [of God to set
his people free] begins to be fulfilled . . . the prayer of
Moses becomes the most striking example of intercessory
prayer, which will be fulfilled in 'the one mediator between
God and men, the man Christ Jesus' (1 Tm 2:5)."[3] This is
a significant statement indeed: that Moses is, after Christ
Jesus himself, our best model for prayer. The remainder of
the story of the Exodus relates a number of stories about
the way that Moses prayed, from which we can not only
learn about his relationship with the Lord but also draw
insight for our own struggle to pray more hopefully.

The incident we've just been discussing was not the
only time Moses turned to the Lord to express his frustration and confusion over whether the Lord was still
willing to help his people. Often enough, Moses found
himself in the position of intermediary—the people were
crying out to him in their hunger and thirst and expecting
him to find a solution for them in the middle of the desert.
All that Moses was able to do was to turn to the Lord and
place the people's needs before him, but sometimes he

---

[3]   CCC 2574.

added a word or two about his own needs, his own weariness, as well.

After crossing the Red Sea and journeying through the desert of Sin, the people encamped at Rephidim, where there wasn't any water. They came to Moses to complain and used that most foolish of all lines—which, despite being foolish, appears in the story of the Exodus more than once—"we were better off in Egypt than we are following you out here in the desert." Moses turns to the Lord, as he has done before to ask the Lord for water or for food, but before he puts their request to God, "Moses cried out to the LORD, 'What shall I do with this people? A little more and they will stone me!'" (Ex 17:4).

In another story, recorded in the book of Numbers, when the Israelites were encamped at Taberah, they began to complain about the food they had to eat. They wanted meat, and all they had was the manna that God provided for them each day. We should stop a moment and consider that—*all they had was manna*: that miraculous bread that fell from the sky every morning; that tasted like whatever you liked best; that they didn't have to plant, or raise, or buy. But the Israelites were getting bored with the manna . . . you know, the same old thing, day in, and day out. They were nostalgic for the menu in Egypt: cucumbers and melons, leeks, onions and garlic, and, of course, meat. They may have been slaves there, sure . . . but at least the food was interesting, wasn't it?

In the midst of this silliness, Moses walks about the camp and hears the people crying out at the entrance to their tents. Perhaps this spirit of feeling sorry for themselves is contagious; at any rate, he turns to the Lord and asks,

> "Why do you treat your servant so badly?" Moses asked the LORD. "Why are you so displeased with me that you burden me with all this people? Was it I who conceived all this people? or was it I who gave them birth, that you tell me to carry them at my breast, like a nurse carrying an infant, to the land you have promised under oath to their fathers? Where can I get meat to give to all this people? For they are crying to me, 'Give us meat for our food.' I cannot carry all this people by myself, for they are too heavy for me." (Nm 11:11–14)

And then comes my favorite line in all of the Old Testament: "If this is the way you will deal with me, then please do me the favor of killing me at once, so that I need no longer face my distress" (Nm 11:15).

I have to say again that I am convinced that prayers like this from Moses are not simply venting and don't imply doubts about God's love or protection. On the contrary, in the context, I think they are actually very hopeful prayers—prayers that demonstrate quite well what we have been talking about all along when we have been considering our supernatural vocation—the call that we have received to do something and to be something that goes beyond our natural abilities to achieve on our own. We see crystallized in Moses the kind of attitude that we all need to bring to our vocations: he was perfectly aware from the beginning that the responsibility entrusted to him was beyond his natural capacities, and from the beginning of his mission, he received an assurance of divine help *from God himself.* It is a testimony to his hope that when he is tested, he turns to the Lord and says, in all honesty, "I can't do this, you've got to help me." As we've heard Caryll Houselander note, it's all too tempting to try to look important in those kinds of moments, to try to figure it out for ourselves. Moses doesn't do that. He turns immediately to the Lord and expects—almost demands—that God provide the help that he promised.

And God keeps his promises. In this story about the people complaining over the food, when Moses admits that he is exhausted—that he's about ready to throw in the towel if he has to bear much more of this—God tells him to call together seventy elders from among the people and appoints them to assist Moses in his daily duties of leadership. When Moses cried out to the Lord, afraid that the thirsty Israelites would stone him if he couldn't find water, the Lord provided water from the most unlikely place: from the side of a rock! If we have any lingering unease about Moses and the directness of his prayer, God provides his own evaluation in the fact that he answers Moses's prayer every time, usually with more than Moses asked for.

The book of Exodus remarks that "the Lord used to speak to Moses face to face, as a person speaks to a friend" (Ex 33:11). This description is unique in all the Scriptures, as is the remark the Lord makes later in the same chapter when he tells Moses that "you have found favor with me and you are my intimate friend" (v. 17). "From this intimacy with the faithful God," the Catechism says, "Moses drew strength and determination for his intercession"; that is, for his prayers for the Israelites. "He does not pray for himself but for the people whom God has made his own."[4] We have already seen how Moses presents the people's needs to the Lord; on other occasions, Moses "withstood [God] in the breach to turn back his destroying anger," as the psalmist says, praying on behalf of the people when the Lord threatened to wipe them out.

On these occasions, Moses and the Lord sound not so much like "intimate friends" as like an old married couple—the subtlety and directness of their conversation is striking and ought to make us marvel at just how good God is, that he can draw someone into so close a relationship with himself. The aftermath of the incident of the golden calf is a good example of what I mean. Moses had been with the Lord on Mount Sinai for forty days, and the Israelites, tired of waiting for him to return, made an idol of gold to worship as their leader. The Lord sees their actions and sends Moses to do something about it. "Then the LORD said to Moses: Go down at once because your people, whom you brought out of the land of Egypt, have acted corruptly" (Ex 32:7).

Did you notice the Lord's choice of words here? Go down to *your* people, Moses, whom *you* brought up from Egypt. He does it again in the next chapter, after Moses has pleaded with the Lord not to obliterate the people entirely: "The LORD spoke to Moses: Go! You and the people whom you have brought up from the land of Egypt

---

4   CCC 2577.

are to go up from here to the land about which I swore to Abraham, Isaac, and Jacob I will give to your descendants" (Ex 33:1).

Moses himself adopted a similar tone, you might recall, during the incident from the book of Numbers: Was it *I* who conceived all these people? Was it *I* who gave birth to them? Are they really *my* responsibility, in other words? The difference is that, surely, God *has* made a promise to be with his people—he has in fact made a covenant with them that they will be *his* people and that he will be *their* God, who is always with them. The Israelites are not acting like his people, to be sure: they have committed the terribly grave sin of idolatry and broken the first commandment of the covenant. But when God begins to speak to Moses as if the people only belonged to him, and not to the Lord, Moses definitely responds.

First, he pleads with the Lord, imploring him to spare the people who have sinned so terribly. He challenges the Lord to do this for his own sake, if not for that of the people: "Why should the Egyptians say, 'With evil intent he brought them out, that he might kill them in the mountains and wipe them off the face of the earth'? Turn from your burning wrath; change your mind about punishing your people" (Ex 32:12).

Most importantly, Moses insists, God made a covenant with Abraham to lead his descendants to the land he promised to him. If he destroys the Israelites here, that promise cannot be fulfilled.

Next, the Lord tells Moses that he will spare the people and allow them to go to the Promised Land and will even provide an angel to protect them but that he himself will not go with them. Moses insists that if the Lord will not go with them, then they will not go. He knows that he is not able to lead the people by himself; he does not know the way, but he does know that he lacks the strength. "If you are not going yourself," he says to God, "do not make us go up from here" (Ex 33:15).

I think we can agree that it is not easy to look the omnipotent Creator of the universe in the eye and tell him that you think he's making a big mistake. The extraordinary way in which Moses speaks to the Lord in these moments of intercession is striking if for no other reason than that so few people, it seems, would have the nerve to talk to God that way. So where does he get the strength to do it? Moses remembers the promises that God has made, and he simply acknowledges them as true and has a full and clear expectation that God will do likewise. He is attached, we might say, to the three firm convictions that we heard Pope John Paul I mention a few chapters back: "God is all-powerful. God loves me immensely. God keeps his promises." Moses's boldness doesn't come from any idea of his own about what he thinks God ought to do. He simply expects God to do what he already said he would do. His prayer, in other words, is an act of hope.

"The arguments of his prayer," the Catechism says, "will inspire the boldness of the great intercessors among the Jewish people and in the Church: God is love; he is therefore righteous and faithful; he cannot contradict himself; he must remember his marvelous deeds, since his glory is at stake, and he cannot forsake this people that bears his name."[5] I don't know how many of us feel like "great intercessors," but we can all learn from Moses to be bolder, or at least more confident, in our prayers. For confidence in prayer is different than presumption; confident prayer is full of hope, for it strives to see things from God's perspective and to pray accordingly. Confident prayer starts from the realization that everything depends on God, and not on me, and that God knows that. Confident prayer believes that if God has a plan in mind for me, a path marked out for me to walk, then he has already considered all the little details of that plan and knows what he's going to do about them. Confident prayer means that if God is true (which he is) and just (which he is), then I have a reason and a right to expect him to do what he said he would do and to keep his word. Confident prayer means that if, at the end of the day, I can look God in the eye and say that I've done everything in my power to understand his plan and to do his will, then I keep looking him in the eye and say, "But this was your idea, and you have to figure it out." Confident, hopeful prayer doesn't resent the fact that my success comes from God and not from me . . . it counts on it.

Moses had an extraordinary ability to pray with confidence, which came about in large part, to be sure, from his extraordinary experiences of the Lord's closeness and the Lord's power. He is an important model for us of what it means to be able to pray with honesty, in all emotional circumstances, and to pray confidently for the Lord's help. But in many ways, the particular closeness that Moses

---

5   CCC 2577.

shared with the Lord is not the norm. Next, we will learn from the experience of an outstanding woman who radiated the love of God to everyone she met, who nonetheless spent most of her life feeling very distant from him. If she can teach us how to pray with hope, we will certainly be prepared for whatever may come our way.

Staying Hopeful When God Hides—
Saint Teresa of Calcutta

Although she is immediately identified with the Indian subcontinent, the woman known to the world as "Mother Teresa" was born some four thousand miles away in Skopje, Albania. Agnes Gonxha Bojaxhiu—her name in Albanian means "little flower" or "rosebud"—was the youngest of her siblings and was born on August 26, 1910. After her father died, when Agnes was eight, her mother raised the children as Roman Catholic. Agnes was devoted to God from an early age and often spoke later in life of having been fascinated as a child by stories of missionaries, especially those like Saint Francis Xavier who served in India and Bengal.

By the time she was twelve, she said, she was convinced that she was being called to serve the Lord as a religious sister. She asked to be admitted to the Sisters of Loreto, an Irish missionary community founded in the nineteenth century, which Agnes knew was active in education and evangelization in India. She traveled first to Loreto Abbey in Rathfarnham, Ireland, to learn English, and then was sent to India in 1929 to begin her novitiate (her training for life in the community). The novitiate was located in Darjeeling, in the Bengal province in northeastern India near the Himalayas; here she learned the Bengali language and taught at Saint Teresa's School. At the end of her novitiate, she professed her first vows as a Sister of Loreto, choosing the name Sister Teresa, after Saint Thérèse of Lisieux, the Carmelite nun who is the patron saint of missionaries—and who, by the way, is also called a "little flower."

Soon Sister Teresa was reassigned to the Entally neighborhood in the eastern part of Calcutta, the capital of Bengal province (now the state of West Bengal). It was in Calcutta that she professed her solemn vows on May 14, 1937; at that point, by the tradition of her community, she became known as "Mother" Teresa. She taught at Saint Mary's School, Entally, which served the daughters of the well-to-do families in the city, for almost twenty years, becoming headmistress of the school in 1944. She was much beloved by the girls and their families and had a positive impact on the life of the school and the community. All in all, she felt confident that she had found her vocation.

Like all Religious, Mother Teresa was required to set aside several days each year for some time away from regular responsibilities to reflect and pray in quiet—her annual retreat. In early September 1946, she had arranged to travel from Calcutta to the community's convent in Darjeeling to make this retreat; on the train on September 10—a journey of about four hundred miles—something happened that would change her life dramatically. Mother Teresa was always very reserved about what exactly took place, but in general terms, she revealed that she felt God calling her, clearly and distinctly, to a new way of serving him. She explains:

> It was a call within my vocation. It was a second calling. It was a vocation to give up even Loreto where I was very happy and to go out in the streets to serve the poorest of the poor. I heard the call to give up all and follow Him into the slums—to serve Him in the poorest of the poor. . . . I knew that it was His will and that I had to follow Him. There was no doubt that it was going to be His work.[6]

Later, Mother Teresa would refer to September 10, 1946 as "Inspiration Day," the true beginnings of what was to become her life's work. It was also the beginning of a period of mystical experiences that lasted for approximately a year and half; during this time, she frequently heard the voice of Jesus speaking to her, a phenomenon called *inner locutions*.

The Lord revealed to her, she said, the depths of his thirst for the love of men and women, especially that he should be known and loved by the poor, but for this to happen, he needed someone to bring his Gospel to the poor and to lead them to him. He addressed Mother Teresa in tender terms, calling her "My own little one," and insisted, over and over, "Come, come, carry me into the holes of

---

[6]   Mother Teresa to Malcom Muggeridge, quoted in Mother Teresa, *Come, Be My Light: The Private Writings of "The Saint of Calcutta,"* ed. Brian Kolodiejchuk, M.C. (New York: Doubleday, 2007), 40.

the poor. Come, be my light."[7] During her retreat and in the months that followed, Mother Teresa kept a record of these locutions, notes of "what went on between Him and me during the days of much prayer."[8]

Returning to Calcutta in October, Mother Teresa was anxious for a chance to see Father Celeste Van Exem, a Jesuit priest who had been her spiritual director since 1944. She immediately told him about the inspiration that she had received on September 10 and that she was convinced that it meant a new way of life for her, bringing Jesus into the lives of the poor by serving them in their own homes and communities. She also told him about the messages she had been receiving from Jesus in the intervening weeks. She trusted his judgment and discernment to help her to understand whether all of this was authentic and truly what God wanted her to do. She resigned herself to receiving his decision and interpretation of her inspirations as an expression of the Will of God for her.

Father Van Exem's first response was to advise her to put the whole affair out of her mind for a time. Mother Teresa, recalling this later to her superior, says that Father did not doubt that the inspiration came from God; nevertheless, she says, "he forbade me even to think about it."[9] This is not unusual advice in the spiritual tradition; often a first step in discerning what comes from God from one's own wishes is simply not to think about it for a while. If the thought goes away, it was just a passing desire; if

---

7   Quoted in *Come, Be My Light*, 42.

8   Ibid.

9   Ibid., 46.

it comes back persistently, this can be a reason to look at it more closely. From October through the following January, however, Mother Teresa continually sought his permission to write to Ferdinand Périer, the archbishop of Calcutta, to lay all of her plans before him and seek his permission to proceed. He finally did give permission—or at least admitted that he didn't think he could stop her—and on January 13, 1947, Mother Teresa wrote the first of many letters to the archbishop explaining her plans for the new congregation.

The next few years would bring more hardship than Mother Teresa could have expected. The archbishop thought her initial letter was too hasty, too forward, and wasn't quite sure what to make of this nun that wanted to leave her convent after so long and start a work with the poor that no one had ever done before. Many letters passed back and forth between Mother Teresa and the archbishop, and between her and her superiors in the Sisters of Loreto—some of which display a bit of apprehension about whether it was an appropriate thing for Mother Teresa to do what she was proposing. At one point, Father Van Exem told her to "drop it for all eternity"[10] unless and until either he or the archbishop should bring up the project with her again.

Finally, after a great deal of deliberation and prayer, Archbishop Périer wrote to the superior of the Sisters of Loreto to say that he would give permission for Mother Teresa to begin the project she was proposing. He came to the convent in Calcutta on January 6, 1948, and after Mass,

---

[10]   Ibid., 78.

he met Mother Teresa to tell her, "You may go ahead."[11] It would be eight more months of seeking permissions from her superiors in the Order and from the Sacred Congregation for Religious, in Rome, before Mother Teresa would be allowed to leave and begin her new work. On August 17, 1948, she did just that: clothed not in a typical religious habit but in a white *sari*—the traditional dress of Indian women—and with just five rupees in her pocket, she set out to do what the Lord had asked of her. She took a course with the Medical Mission Sisters and found a temporary home with the Little Sisters of the Poor in Calcutta; both of these experiences taught her valuable skills for tending the sick and dying. On December 21 she began to put those skills into practice as she started her rounds of visiting the slums of Calcutta to bring the light of Christ into the homes of the poor and the abandoned.

After attending Mass and receiving Holy Communion each morning, Mother Teresa went out, with her rosary in her hand, to visit poor people and families in their homes, to nurse the sick, to feed the hungry, and to care for the dying, most of whom she found lying in the streets. Over the next few months, some of her former students from Saint Mary's began to join her in her work—to wear the white and blue sari and come to live with her. They established a school and later on a hospice to tend to the sick and dying poor and to help them to receive the sacraments and to prepare for death; many more such institutions would follow wherever the Sisters were.

On October 7, 1950, the *Missionaries of Charity* were

---

[11]   Ibid., 105.

officially recognized by the archbishop of Calcutta as a religious order; by the end of the decade, they were being sent to found convents and serve the poor in other parts of India, and by 1965, they had opened a house in Venezuela. This was followed quickly by foundations in Rome and eventually on every continent; in each place, the Sisters keep scrupulously their fourth vow, to serve the Lord by caring for "the poorest of the poor." Today, more than 4,500 Missionaries of Charity serve in 133 countries around the world.

Mother Teresa quickly won renown for her work with the poor and suffering, beginning with the *Padma Shri*, India's third-highest civilian honor, in 1962 and culminating with her being honored with the Nobel Peace Prize in 1979. (She declined the typical ceremonial banquet and asked that the funds set aside for it—about $200,000—be used to help the poor in India.) She was honored by many national governments on various occasions, including in the United States, where she received the Presidential Medal of Freedom in 1985 and was made an honorary citizen in 1996—becoming one of only seven people to have received this privilege and one of the two to have been thus honored during his or her lifetime. When she died on September 5, 1997, she was granted a state funeral by the government of India in recognition of her services to the poor of all religions. The cause for her canonization was begun very quickly—Pope John Paul II waived the usual five-year waiting period before such a process is allowed to begin—and Mother Teresa was beatified on October 19, 2003.

Mother Teresa had become such a world figure in the second half of the twentieth century that it's safe to say that her story as we've described it so far was known to just about everybody, at least in its broad strokes. As the Missionaries of Charity spread, Mother Teresa would be invited to visit the Congregation's houses and ministries around the world; she also received countless invitations to address conferences, gatherings of priests, and even joint sessions of Congress. Everywhere she went, people were impressed and consoled by the cheerfulness that was always evident in this little nun, who worked so hard in such difficult conditions and had seen such great suffering and deprivation for so long. It seems to most people as if she were always smiling.

Outwardly, of course, she was. In the years since her death, though, we have come to understand a different facet of Mother Teresa's spiritual life, one that she kept very private and only confided in a few trusted priests, her spiritual directors, during her lifetime. I mentioned how the six months or so following "Inspiration Day"—the tenth of October 1946—was a period of intense closeness with the Lord for Mother Teresa: inner locutions and other mystical experiences were part of her life quite regularly and reassured her that she was on the right path. But then, right around the time when the work of the Missionaries of Charity began, the entire atmosphere changed—Mother Teresa's relationship with God had suddenly gone dark. The first time that she mentioned it in writing was in 1953 in a letter to Archbishop Périer: "Your Grace, Please pray specially for me that I may not spoil His work and that

Our Lord may show Himself—for there is such terrible darkness within me, as if everything was dead. It has been like this more or less from the time I started "the work." Ask Our Lord to give me courage."[12]

Some years later, in a letter to her spiritual director at the time, Father Joseph Neuner, she gives a more complete picture of what the "terrible darkness" meant for her:

> The work started—in Dec. 1948.—By 1950 as the number of the Sisters grew—the work grew.—
>
> Now Father—since 49 or 50 this terrible sense of loss—this untold darkness—this loneliness—this continual longing for God—which gives me that pain deep down in my heart.—Darkness is such that I really do not see—neither with my mind nor with my reason.—The place of God in my soul is blank.—There is no God in me.—When the pain of longing is so great—I just long & long for God— and then it is that I feel—He does not want me—He is not there.[13]

This very intense, very personal struggle in the life of Mother Teresa came as a shock to many people when it was brought to light a few years after her death. During her lifetime, Mother kept very quiet about it, revealing it only to a few trusted priests, mostly in confession and in that confidential relationship known as spiritual direction. What evidence exists of it comes in the form of a few

---

[12]   Ibid., 149.

[13]   Ibid., 210–11.

journals that she kept during retreats and from letters that she wrote to her spiritual directors—which she asked them to destroy once they had read them. Of course, recognizing Mother Teresa's obvious holiness, they held on to the letters and presented them to the Church as evidence in the process of considering her for canonization as a saint; it is in relation to this process that they have become known and were prepared for publication. In 2007, the postulator of her cause for canonization edited Mother's private correspondence and compiled the book *Come, Be My Light: The Private Writings of the Saint of Calcutta.*

The reaction to the news of Mother Teresa's inner darkness was mixed: some people wondered how she could have done everything that she did—such works of charity, such tremendous efforts to spread the faith and lead people to God—when she herself spent nearly fifty years feeling that God was not directly involved in her daily life, that he had forgotten about her and did not want anything to do with her. In one particularly nasty attack, the British journalist and self-described "anti-theist" Christopher Hitchens—who had long been one of Mother Teresa's most vocal critics—described her as "a confused old lady who [the Church] knew had for all practical purposes ceased to believe."[14] It seems that at some level Mother herself might not have been so dismissive of this judgment; she wrote in 1962 to Bishop Lawrence Picachy, who had once been her spiritual director: "People say they are drawn closer to God—seeing my strong faith.—Is this

---

14   Christopher Hitchens, "Teresa, Bright and Dark," *Newsweek*, 28 August 2007.

not deceiving people? Every time I have wanted to tell the truth—"that I have no faith"—the words just do not come—my mouth remains closed.—And yet I keep on smiling at God and all."[15]

It seems safe to say, in other words, that Mother Teresa herself was not quite sure what to make of this mysterious darkness that had taken hold of her. She did know several things for certain: where it must have come from and what she was going to do about it. She had long ago given God free rein in her life—in fact, in April 1942, after long deliberation and discussion with her spiritual director, she had made a private vow; she wanted to give God something very beautiful, she said, and so she made a solemn promise to him, never, ever to refuse him anything he should ask of her. Although she did not understand the purpose for the terrible loneliness that she felt, because she experienced this separation from God, her faith told her that it must be his will for her. And because she believed that it was what he wanted, she was determined to accept it willingly. "I accept whatever He gives," she wrote, "and I give whatever He takes."[16]

And it is this acceptance and this underlying faith in God's will and God's providence that allows us to answer Mother Teresa's critics and to understand a little bit of what was happening in her life. It also allows us to see how her struggles, intimately personal and unique as they are, can guide us and give us insight into our own efforts to pray with greater trust and hope.

---

[15]   Quoted in *Come, Be My Light,* 238.

[16]   Ibid.

First of all, is it true to say that Mother Teresa had really lost faith—that she had really ceased to believe? The Church certainly doesn't think so—the popes are not in the habit of beatifying people who have no faith!—and so we have to interpret carefully Mother's expressions. It is a good lesson for us—it is important to remember that faith and feelings are not the same thing, that in fact they can often be quite different and directed at quite different objects. We have seen this demonstrated in several instances already: Blessed Pier Giorgio had faith in God's plan for his vocation, even as he felt very distraught at the loss of a potential relationship; Blessed Chiara Luce believed that God had sent her her illness "at the right time" even as the reality of surgery and treatment must have frightened her. Writing to Father Neuner in 1967, Mother Teresa herself noted the difference between what she felt—and expressed in her letters—and what she really believed: "My thoughts are only the Sisters & the Poor. . . . They are my prayer, they are my very life.—I love them as I love Jesus—& now as I do not love Jesus—I do not love them either. I know this is only feelings—for my will is steadfast bound to Jesus & so to the Sisters & the Poor."[17]

Like Moses crying out to the Lord in the midst of his exhaustion and frustration, Mother Teresa often gives voice to her feelings of loneliness and abandonment in her letters. As we saw in the case of Moses, this is not merely venting or complaining but a sign of humility and honesty. Time and time again, one realizes that the reason Mother Teresa feels the darkness so keenly is not that

---

[17]   Ibid., 257.

she thinks that she is so special that she should always have visions and locutions—that she is somehow entitled to special heights of mysticism because she has done something great for God—but quite the opposite: because she is convinced that she cannot do anything without him, and she is distressed at the thought that she is in any way apart from him. She is pained by his absence because she knows that she needs him so much.

So we see that it isn't possible to say that Mother Teresa has lost her faith; if she didn't believe that God existed, she wouldn't worry about whether he was in her life. She hasn't lost her love; she loves God so deeply and sincerely that his apparent absence from her gives her tremendous pain. And she hasn't stopped hoping in him, either. Theological hope is that habitual trust that our ability to fulfill our supernatural vocation comes from God alone. Mother was convinced of this above all else—it was, in fact, the one thing that she never doubted:

> [If uncertainty remains] that's the time to go on your knees, eh? . . . In that prayer, God cannot deceive you because that prayer comes from within you. That is the time you want Him most. Once you have got God within you, that's for life. There is no doubt. You can have other doubts, eh? But that particular one will never come again. No, I have never had doubt. . . . But I am convinced that it is He and not I. That it is His work, and not my work. I am only at His disposal. Without Him I can do nothing.[18]

---

18   Ibid., 260.

Mother Teresa and her spiritual directors saw it as significant that the darkness began around the time that she started her work as a Missionary of Charity. For one thing, it seemed to be a necessary part of that work; as Father Michael van der Peet, who first met Mother in 1975, described it, "the reason Mother Teresa had to undergo so much darkness in her life is that it would bring about a greater identification with the poor,"[19] who themselves experience such tremendous loneliness and isolation. We have talked about the ways in which hope allows us to recognize the love of Christ, who eases our loneliness by identifying with us in our moments of abandonment. It seems that the Lord was asking Mother Teresa to become like him even in his feelings of being abandoned by the Father so that she could participate in this ministry of consoling the lonely with Christ's own love.

As a result, Mother found consolation in the visits that she made to the homes and neighborhoods of those she served as a Missionary of Charity—all the consolation that she sought but could not find in quiet prayer alone with Jesus. When she was among the poor and suffering, and knew that she was encountering Christ in them, she could talk to him there in ways for which she did not have the words at other times: "When outside—in the work— or meeting people—there is a presence—of somebody living very close—in very me.—I don't know what this is—but very often even every day—that love in me for

---

[19]   Ibid., 269.

God grows more real.—I find myself telling Jesus unconsciously most strange tokens of love."[20]

Because she had not lost hope, Mother Teresa was able to see these daily encounters with the Lord as something meaningful and real, as a true way of making contact with him, and responding to the longing that was there, "deep down somewhere in [her] heart." Was it the kind of prayer she experienced in those six months after her "Inspiration Day"? No, clearly not. Was it the easily-flowing meditation that she was able to do for hours in her early days in the convent? No, even that did not come any more: "I don't pray any longer. [*she wrote in a letter to Jesus in 1959*]—I utter words of community prayers—and try my utmost to get out of every word the sweetness it has to give.—But my prayer of union is not there any longer.—I no longer pray.—My soul is not one with You."[21]

And to Father Neuner: "Before I could spend Hours before Our Lord—loving Him—talking to Him—and now—not even meditation goes properly—nothing but "My God"—even that sometimes does not come."[22]

But the fact that her prayers are not easy, that they do not come spontaneously, that they are not poetic, none of this overshadows one essential, all-important fact: throughout these fifty years, when Mother Teresa feels horribly alone and abandoned, *she never stops praying.*

This is the sign that hope is at work in her heart. As we have heard Mother Teresa say already, never along

---

[20]   Ibid., 211.

[21]   Ibid., 193

[22]   Ibid., 211.

this long path of suffering has she doubted that God was with her, although he has withdrawn the signs of his presence, and so she continues to communicate with him, even when he does not seem to respond. Early on, she described her response to God in this situation as "smiling at him"; in an undated letter she wrote to God at Father Picachy's request, she tells him, "Here I am Lord, with joy I accept all to the end of life—& I will smile at Your Hidden Face—always."[23]

Your hidden face. The virtue of hope allowed Mother Teresa to trust that God was present even when she could not see him or sense his closeness, to accept that he was near, even if he were hiding from her. And so she smiled in his direction, trusting that he could see her, even if she could not see him. It reminds me of the response we heard from Matt Talbot when someone asked him what he prayed about all day in front of the tabernacle: "Oh, I just look at him," he said, speaking of Jesus present in the Blessed Sacrament, "and he looks at me." The mystery of the Eucharist sustained Mother Teresa as well throughout the decades of her inner darkness and strengthened her hope in Christ's hidden presence in her midst.

To hold on to her faith in the Real Presence involved repeated acts of trust and hope, as she confided in Father Neuner: "From my childhood I have had a most tender love for Jesus in the Blessed Sacrament—but this too has gone.—I feel nothing before Jesus—and yet I would not miss Holy [Communion] for anything."[24] Yet the Sisters

---

[23]   Ibid., 188.

[24]   Ibid., 211.

who lived with her testified to her great reverence for the Blessed Sacrament throughout her life, and a story from her old age demonstrates touchingly just what the Presence of Christ meant to her. Father Gary, a priest of the Missionaries of Charity, relates:

> Mother had the grace in the latter years, to have the Blessed Sacrament in her hospital room, and she always wanted it with her. . . . [In August 1996] she had another heart failure right before our eyes. A tube was put down into her lungs to assist her breathing and relieve the pressure upon her heart.
>
> Before the tubes were finally removed, [the doctor] . . . said, "Father, go home and bring that box to Mother." For a second I wondered, "what box— [a] shoe box?" He said, "That box, that temple they bring and put in her room and Mother looks at it all the time. If you bring it and put it in the room Mother will become so quiet." I realized he meant the tabernacle with the Blessed Sacrament. He said to me, "When that box is there, in the room, she is just looking and looking and looking at that box." The Hindu doctor was an unknowing witness to the power of the Eucharist over our Mother.[25]

Here we see one more secret of Mother Teresa's holiness, one more sign of the workings of hope in her life, and one that we can learn to imitate in our own spiritual journeys and lives of faith as well. "She is just looking

---

[25] Ibid., 328.

and looking and looking" at Jesus, the doctor said, without really knowing it, and if there were ever a better description of a habitual disposition of soul, of a virtue, than that, I think we would be hard-pressed to come up with it. Hope, of course, is the theological virtue that keeps us looking and looking at Jesus, and at the goal that Jesus sets for us, while we are on the way to him. In Mother Teresa's life, the fact that she found him in the Blessed Sacrament *and* in others is significant, for recognizing him in each place required an act of trust.

In the sick, in the disfigured, in the dirty, in those eaten up by disease, Jesus doesn't look like himself. In the desperate, in those who do what they have to do to survive, in those whom society has marginalized, and who have responded by keeping others at arm's length, Jesus doesn't look like himself. In those who lie and cheat and steal, in those who have hurt us, or who take advantage of us, or come to us with an agenda, Jesus doesn't look like himself. But then again, in the sacred Host, a small, thin piece of unleavened Bread, Jesus doesn't look like himself either. Mother Teresa trusted that he was there in the Host for one reason, *because he said he would be*. And she went to seek him in all of those she served for the same one reason: because he said he would be there as well. Theological hope allowed her to trust that although she felt personally abandoned, she was never truly alone— that Jesus was with her in some mysterious, hidden way. Why? Because he said he would be.

Repeated acts of looking and looking and looking at him in the tabernacle and in others gave Mother Teresa the strength and hope to keep seeking him in her own soul as well without losing heart, even though for five decades she found him there very infrequently. We can— we must—admire and imitate the works of charity that Mother Teresa carried out. But we must also strive to learn from her experience and her example the importance of repeated acts of hope and trust—even when our hearts are burdened by pain and sorrow—which allow us to recognize the presence of God in our lives and his plan for us.

Conclusion—Acts of Hope

Throughout this book, we've had the opportunity to become acquainted with some extraordinary men and women and to encounter them at the incredibly poignant, dramatic moments in their lives. I trust you have been as impressed and moved as I have been by their stories and their experiences—and not only touched emotionally, but encouraged and enlightened by the ways in which their individual lives draw out the truth that is common to the vocation that every disciple shares—the supernatural call to greatness that is common to every human being and that is the reason and the object of our hope. Now it is time for us to decide whether we can apply the lessons we've learned from these heroes of hope to our own lives and try to join them "on the way" that leads to our eternal goal.

Let's return for a moment to where we started these discussions, to the definition of a virtue as a habitual tendency to do some good thing. When we're talking about the theological virtue of hope, remember, the "theological" part of that phrase means that it has been infused into us at Baptism along with the gift of sanctifying grace. We've got it . . . so far, so good. But the "virtue" part of the name means that we've got to do something with it! Virtues, however they are acquired, need to be developed in practice; if we've got it, we've got to use it. Our hope isn't going to do us any good, and it isn't going to get any stronger or be evident in our lives, unless we are exercising it—making what are usually called "acts of hope."

So we have a few questions to consider if we are going to make these acts of hope effectively. First, *when* do we make acts of hope? The easy answer is: all the time. Because the goal toward which theological hope is leading us is eternal life, and one necessary prerequisite for attaining eternal life is dying in this world in order to go to the next, then as long as we are still here, we're are still "on the way" to the goal. As we have seen, hope is the virtue of people "on the way," and to live hopefully gives context and purpose to life in this broken world of ours. It keeps our eyes fixed on heaven, it prioritizes our earthly needs and desires according to God's plan, and it reminds us that God will be our help in the midst of daily trials. The more we are consciously mindful of these things— the more we keep heaven in our sights—the easier it is to live day by day without losing heart.

Thus, we should be living with a general attitude of hopefulness and making sure that words of hope are part of our daily prayers. (For that matter, we should start by making sure we are praying daily.) But from time to time we will need to make more deliberate acts of hope, and

these come at rather specific moments. The British Catholic author G. K. Chesterton explains how important it is
to remember exactly what hope is for: "As long as matters
are really hopeful, hope is a mere flattery or platitude; it is
only when everything is hopeless that hope begins to be a
strength at all. Like all the Christian virtues, it is as unrea-
sonable as it is indispensable. . . . The more hopeless is the
situation the more hopeful must be the man."[26]

In other words, God gives us hope, like all the virtues,
because we need it, and we must use it more when we
need it more, although these are the times when we may
be tempted to use it less. For in situations when we are
frightened, or feel abandoned, or are overwhelmed by
temptations or sin—in all these situations and more when
we are emotionally and spiritually exhausted—usually the
first thing to go is our desire or what we consider our ability to pray. Perhaps we can't muster the energy, or perhaps
we think God doesn't want to hear from us. Perhaps, on
the other hand, we know that if we pray and ask for help,
the answer will be a command to do something that will
involve more suffering, or a change or a challenge we are
not ready to face. In any case, what is needed in these
moments, as we have seen, is to pray more, not less—to
make deliberate acts of hope *because* the situation seems
hopeless. It is possible to do this if we keep in mind that
God already knows all the things that threaten to keep us
from praying. We can mention them in prayer—tell him
we are afraid (like Caryll Houselander) or exhausted (like

---

[26]   G. K. Chesterton, *Heretics* (New York: John Lane Co., 1912),
        119, 129.

Moses) or out of our element (like Joseph Freinademetz) or heartsick (like Pier Giorgio Frasatti) and know that he will understand.

We should keep in mind, too, speaking of timing, what it means to pray for hope, relative to situations that require us to be and act hopefully. For in these cases, our actions must be suited to our petitions. In other words, if we are going to pray with confidence, then we must trust God not only to hear our prayers, and to know what's best in regard to them, but then trust him actually to *do* what he said he would do *at the time that he knows best*. But this does not mean that we sit or kneel and pray for hope or courage or strength for a given situation and then stay where we are until we begin to *feel* hopeful and courageous and strong. No . . . we make our prayer—we pray with confidence—and then we get up and go and face the situation about which we were praying—the one that requires hope and strength and courage—and rely on God to give us the grace that we need *at the time that we need it*. This in itself requires hope and trust, and so we see again the habitual nature of this virtue. Hope builds on hope: but every time that God answers our prayers, we have a greater reason to hope the next time we pray, provided that we are mindful enough to pay attention and recognize what he is doing.

Now that we are beginning to understand *when* we should make acts of hope, we can also ask *how* we are to do it. As we have come to understand, there are as many ways to make an act of hope as there are people and situations—from the simple, plaintive, "My God" that was all that Mother Teresa was able to get out most days in the chapel, to the twenty-five minutes that Chiara Luce spent talking things over with Jesus, to the beautiful prayer of contrition and repentance that won God's forgiveness over and over for the brother in Saint Amphilóchios's story. As all of our heroes of hope teach us, a sincere cry from the heart asking for God's help to take the next step along the way that he has marked out for us is as good an act of hope as we can ever make.

There are, though, some time-tested ways of praying for hope that the Church offers for our consideration. One is a traditional daily prayer—called, unsurprisingly, the Act of Hope—that is found in many prayer books and in the *Compendium of the Catechism of the Catholic Church*. It serves not just as an easily-memorized formula that can be prayed alone or in a group but also as a kind of miniature catechesis on what the theological virtue of hope is and how it works. Each of its lines has something to teach us about the nature and the reasons for our hope.

"O Lord God," it begins, and reminds us that the reason that we can hope at all is that God has given us access, that he allows us to call on him, as he promised Moses at the burning bush when he revealed his sacred Name, "Lord," and said that he heard the cry of his people. "O Lord God, I hope by your grace"—because everything that we hope for comes from God's initiative and not our own—"for the pardon of all my sins," since ongoing conversion and forgiveness is a necessary part of staying "on the way" that God has marked out for us, and only he can make that possible for us. "And after life here," the prayer goes on, "to gain eternal happiness," since, as we have seen many times, it is this beatitude which puts all of our earthly joys and goals in their proper order. The prayer then reveals the reasons for our hope: "because you have promised it, who are infinitely powerful, faithful, kind and merciful"—here we see again those three firm convictions we heard about from Pope John Paul I: God is all-powerful, God loves us immensely, God keeps his promises . . . and this is why we can hope in him. Finally, we respond to God's goodness with our own commitment: "In this hope I intend to live and die"—what we see with eyes of hope marks out the path for us, and the strength that comes from God, in whom we trust, gives us the ability to stay on the way and to love him to the end.

Other vocal prayers also express our hope and trust in God. Especially important are the Psalms, those inspired prayers in the Word of God, that are given to us by God himself so that we will have the words we need to address him. Some psalms are full of joy and praise God for his faithfulness from start to finish. Others are not so straightforward, at first glance, but for that reason might be more consoling in the long run. Imagine the state of mind the psalmist must have been in to have written dramatic words like these: "Save me, God, for the waters have reached my neck. I have sunk into the mire of the deep, where there is no foothold. I have gone down to the watery depths; the flood overwhelms me" (Ps 69:2–3). As I mentioned when we were talking about Moses and his prayer, we're not used to hearing this kind of language addressed to God, but in reality, there are quite a few psalms that take a similar tone, called *psalms of lament*. In fact, Jesus quotes from one of them on the Cross, reciting the first line of Psalm 22 when he cries out, "My God, my God, why have you forsaken me?" (Mk 15:34).

Psalms of lament are perfect for people in desperate situations because they begin with rather dramatic, sometimes rather lengthy descriptions of all the trouble and strife that the psalmist finds himself in, and like some of our heroes of hope have taught us, the psalmist puts all of his emotions and all of his needs right where they need to be: in God's hands. And then, invariably, toward the middle of a psalm of lament, the same thing always happens: the psalmist recalls something that the Lord has done, either for himself or for his people, or he recalls some aspect of the Lord's power and goodness. And his response is the same: he accepts this realization as one more reason to trust the Lord, even in the midst of the dire situation, reasoning that if God has been good in the past, he can and will be good to him again. Thus every psalm of lament becomes an act of hope—and people with reasons to cry out to the Lord in lamentation can benefit by reading these psalms all the way through.

Besides these more or less formal prayers, we are expressing our hope every time we perform other acts of Christian virtue, since these are all related to keeping us on the way toward our eternal goal, and it is ultimately hope that keeps that goal in view. Whenever we treat another person with kindness and compassion, welcoming him or her in the name of Christ, we greet him as a fellow traveler on the way and make not just an act of charity but also an act of hope in the communion of saints that finds its ultimate fulfillment in the kingdom of heaven. Each time we put aside ambition or worldly things, asking the Lord to protect us from useless thoughts and desires, we are practicing not just humility and detachment but also making acts of hope, which judges the things of the world in reference to eternal life and rejects whatever is an obstacle to that goal. Our participation in the sacraments is likewise an act of faith and of hope. To humbly confess our sins and seek forgiveness and penance acknowledges our need for conversion and the grace that keeps us on the way and prevents us from falling into presumption and despair. And frequent, humble, worthy reception of Jesus Christ in the Holy Eucharist expresses our hopeful trust that he will sustain us on our journey through this life until we reach the fulfillment of our hope and definitive, everlasting communion with him.

Communion with him! No matter how ugly the world may seem—no matter how broken and bent society may get, no matter how difficult the circumstances of our daily lives—this one fact remains unchanging: the almighty triune God has created you and me *for communion with him!* We are made for it. We are destined to it. He has given us the virtue of theological hope, together with the other virtues, to make sure that we can attain it. And he has given us the witness of so many holy men and women, so many heroes of hope, to inspire and to guide us, to show us the path that leads to our destiny, that leads to him. Now we too must respond to this call to greatness; we too must be heroic. Now we too must dare to hope.